AF581168

Beauvoir and Her Sisters

Beauvoir and Her Sisters

The Politics of Women's Bodies in France

SANDRA REINEKE

UNIVERSITY OF ILLINOIS PRESS

Urbana, Chicago, and Springfield

© 2011 by the Board of Trustees
of the University of Illinois
All rights reserved
Manufactured in the United States of America
C 5 4 3 2 1
∞ This book is printed on acid-free paper.

Library of Congress Cataloging-in-Publication Data
Reineke, Sandra.
Beauvoir and her sisters : the politics of women's
bodies in France / Sandra Reineke.
p. cm.
Includes bibliographical references and index.
ISBN-13: 978-0-252-03619-4 (hbk. : alk. paper)
ISBN-10: 0-252-03619-0 (hbk. : alk. paper)
1. Feminism—France—History—20th century.
2. Feminist literature—France—History and criticism.
3. Citizenship—France.
4. Women—Political activity—France.
5. Women—Sexual behavior—France.
6. Women—Identity.
7. Beauvoir, Simone de, 1908–1986—Criticism
and interpretation.
I. Title.
HQ1617.R43 2012
305.420944—dc22 2010046892

To Julien and Adrien.

CONTENTS

ACKNOWLEDGMENTS

MY WORK ON THIS BOOK has benefited from the help and support of many individuals, institutions, and research facilities. At Indiana University, where this study was conceived, I wish to thank my mentor, Jean C. Robinson, who inspired, trained, and guided me, as well as the university's librarians, who aided me in hunting down needed materials. I am also thankful to the librarians at the Fashion Institute of Technology in New York, at the Bibliothèque nationale de France and the Bibliothèque Marguerite Durand in Paris, and at the University of Idaho in Moscow, Idaho, where I am now working. I am particularly grateful to Nancy Young, who on many occasions offered her help with finding copies of the women's magazine *Elle* examined for this study.

I am also grateful to my colleagues at the University of Idaho, particularly Kathy Aiken, Don Crowley, John Mihelich, Sarah Nelson, and Debbie Storrs, who have been loyal and supportive advocates of my work and research interests, and Kelli Schrand, whose support is unparalleled. Institutional support came from the University of Idaho Research Office, which provided me with an opportunity to present some of the findings of my study at scholarly conferences. I am indebted to Yolanda A. Patterson, who co-organized the Tenth Simone de Beauvoir Society International Conference in Torino, Italy, in 2002, and Dawn Marley, organizer of the international conference "Francophone Women's Magazines Inside and Outside France" at the University of Surrey in England in 2006. I wish to thank the conference participants for their helpful comments on my papers.

All intellectual work is a process of accumulation. Four individuals, in particular, stand out for me for the way in which their intellectual generosity contributed to my work. I am indebted to Jean C. Robinson, Amy G. Mazur, Rachel G. Fuchs, and Karen Offen, who are also my role models. None of whom, of course, should be held in any way responsible for the results.

Chapters 2 and 3 are revised versions of previously published articles. "Secondary Citizens" appeared in *Simone de Beauvoir Studies* 24 (2007–2008): 32–48 as "Pretty Pictures: Beauvoir's Feminist Critique of French Consumer Culture in *The Second Sex* and *Les Belles Images*" (reprinted by permission). "Citizen Consumers" first appeared in *Contemporary French Civilization* 34, no. 1 (Winter/Spring 2010): 41–72 as "Fashioning Female Citizens: Popular Women's Magazines and Reproductive Rights in Fifth Republic France" (reprinted by permission). I wish to thank the editors of both journals for their aid and support.

At the University of Illinois Press, my editor, Joan Catapano, was an advocate from the beginning, and her patience with and understanding of what proved to be a complex process are truly appreciated. I also wish to thank Tad Ringo, Jane Lyle, and Katherine Jensen for their extra-ordinary assistance.

I also wish to thank my family, Ulla and Hermann Reineke, Ulli Reineke, Susan Quinlan, Terry and Carolyn Quinlan, Erin Quinlan, Derek Peacock, and Deborah and Tom Boza, as well as my friends on two continents, Heike Kreutzberg, Jan and Steffi Bensien, Pascal Gramain, Samir Boukhris, Meredith and Steven Toth, Anne-Marie Fulfer and Sunil Ramalingam, Kim Shaw and Lucas Rate, Deb Stenkamp and Charles Swift, Amanda and Ben Barton, Jessica Ting, Karen Marsh, Tanya Volk, and Kim Windsor for their interest in this project, their support, and their help throughout the years.

Most of all, I wish to thank my husband, Sean M. Quinlan, without whose love, patience, and intellectual feedback I would not have been able to complete this project. Only he knows what I owe him. I am dedicating this book to our two beautiful children, Julien and Adrien, who are a daily source of happiness to us. No words can express our love for them. We hope that they will grow up to live in a world of freedom and gender equality.

INTRODUCTION

THIS BOOK EXAMINES a perennial political question: Are women citizens, and if so, how can they speak and act together politically? Recent research in the area of gender and politics has started to shed light on the questions of when and how women participate in political terms. However, studies in the area of democratic theory and citizenship rights have only begun to address the central question of how citizens make themselves into political agents. Arguably, we can better understand how women participate in the political realm by understanding how female citizens—who are traditionally marginalized from the public and political life—attempt to construct a collective political consciousness or identity that can serve as a springboard for political activism (Childs and Krook 2006; Henderson and Jeydel 2007; see also the section "Recent Scholarship" below).

My study contributes to this important area of research by examining how, in the 1970s, 1980s, and 1990s, French women used reading and writing about women's sexuality and reproductive rights as a vehicle to promote the idea of communities of women, characterized by a collective feminine identity and likely common political interests. As I shall argue, for second-wave women's rights activists in France and elsewhere, the idea of women's communality held great potential for women's political agency in various areas of public policy, including state laws governing reproductive rights.

In this way, this book presents a case study to show how women can come together to create an "imagined sisterhood" (Werbner 1999, 223) so that they can speak and act together in the political realm. I am borrowing from Pnina Werbner's pioneering study on the feminist collective imagination, and applying it to a specific place and time: postwar France. For the purposes of this study, this period spans the years from 1944, when French women first acquired the right to vote, to 1993, when the French state made hindering a woman from obtaining access to abortion a crime, and which includes 1970, the year the French women's liberation movement, the Mouvement de la libération de la femme (MLF), was born. (The name was later changed by the activists to Mouvement de libération des femmes as they signed pamphlets and publications.)

I see France as an important case study in this area of inquiry because French women were enfranchised considerably late in comparison to women elsewhere in the Western Hemisphere, and yet France has a long and powerful history of feminist activism (Offen 1994). When French women finally acquired full active citizenship in 1944 following World War II, they continued to face persisting political and social inequalities. In this book, I am concerned with one of the most striking examples of potentially repressive state legislation: abortion laws. These laws denied women the right to control their own bodies, a right included in the liberal republican ideal of citizenship. In response to these inequalities, French women started a concerted effort to demand reproductive rights for women as part of general citizenship rights. For the purpose of this study, I analyze how women's writing helped constitute "women" politically by articulating, expressing, and disseminating feminist claims for gender equality in postwar France. I identify three different levels of women's writing: high feminist literature, mass popular women's magazines, and feminist reviews.

In short, I have two goals in this book. First, my analysis aims to demonstrate how women's writing helped form an "imagined sisterhood," a community of women with the potential for real political change. Second, I aim to show how the concept of an "imagined sisterhood" enabled women to address issues of female embodiment in postwar French society, especially in terms of how postwar culture constructed the female body as an object of consumer desire rather than a subject of individual citizenship rights.

The Case Context

Like women elsewhere, French women had historically been excluded from citizenship rights, because they were deemed unsuited for politics and civic life owing to their corporeal, or "natural," difference from men. In France, women's exclusion from political participation stemmed mostly from a strong cultural association between women and excess (sexually or otherwise), which classified women and their interests as "particular" and at odds with the common good. In other words, women's activities were considered a threat to the social and political order of the state and bourgeois society (Hertz 1983; Hunt 1992; J. Jones 1996; Tiersten 2001). Viewed in conjunction with the development of modern practices of consumption, which developed alongside the state, women in France were excluded from civic life and participation. In this way, they became objects, not subjects, of political discourse, including laws governing sexuality and reproduction (Accampo, Fuchs, and Stewart 1995; Cova 1997).

Throughout French history, women activists had tried to redress sociopolitical inequalities, but women's push for citizenship rights was complicated by the following theoretical conundrum: Was female equality to be based on women's (bodily) sameness to or difference from men? That question preoccupied French feminist thought throughout history and will be discussed in more detail in chapter 1. Thus, when President Charles de Gaulle finally decreed in 1944 that women were full active citizens with the right to vote, it was not to suggest that women had the same "inalienable" rights as men, but rather to reward them for their participation in the Resistance during World War II (Duchen 1994, 33). Even after 1944, women continued to experience grave social and political inequalities.

By the late 1960s, in the wake of the students' and workers' revolt that had swept through France, women renewed their efforts to articulate demands for women's rights, including access to abortion. Leading in this endeavor was the women's liberation movement, or MLF, which explicitly connected female bodily experience (such as sexuality, motherhood, and abortion) with the struggle against political marginalization. This major feminist concern manifested itself in the movement's preoccupation with reproductive rights. This book, however, is not a study of the MLF. Nor is it a study of the political processes that finally won French women the right to abortion.

Rather, this study investigates a selection of women's writings to show their potential for collective political agency. Thus, all of the texts I examine are examples of women's writing for sociopolitical change, which enabled women to carve out a social space apart from traditional feminine expectations to construct a political community. I have called this social space an "imagined sisterhood" (Werbner 1999, 223), not unlike the imagined communities described by Benedict Anderson (1983) in his study of the cultural construction of national identity. If, as Anderson suggests, modern print media shape our collective imagination as a political community, then women's writing on matters of sexuality and reproduction can be understood as contributing to a politically potent "imagined sisterhood." Arguably, women's sisterhood may represent and promote a collective feminine identity and, potentially, political agency.

Throughout French history, women writers attempted to participate not just in the sharing of personal experiences contained in diaries, autobiographies, and novels, but also in the dissemination of political ideas published in newspapers, journals, and political tracts (DeJean 1991; DeJean and Miller 1991; Preston 1995). Crucially, the burgeoning commercialization of public life in the eighteenth century, particularly the development of commercial print media, enabled a growing number of women to participate in public discourse through the act of reading and writing (Moscovici 2000; Walton 2000; Hesse 2002).

Opportunities for women to take advantage of this new freedom varied from one historical period to another. In postwar France, as part of the larger students' and workers' revolt of the late 1960s, women demanded greater participation in public discourses about what we today call "women's issues," such as sexuality, reproduction, work, and consumption. The women's liberation movement, for instance, published weekly and monthly journals to raise awareness about women's sexuality and reproductive rights.

But it was the publication in 1949 of a controversial study about women's social existence by the French philosopher and novelist Simone de Beauvoir (1908–86), titled *Le Deuxième sexe* (*The Second Sex*), that made it possible, not just for women but for French society as a whole, to engage in discourses about sexuality and reproduction. While Beauvoir's writing in *Le Deuxième sexe* set the tone for women's political activism, the women's liberation movement and its independently published feminist reviews carried out the task of informing women and organizing them into an empowered "sisterhood." Ironically, the reviews' commercial counterpart, the market of women's magazines, which also mushroomed during this period, appropriated the liberal feminist agenda to create its own feminine space, a for-profit, glossy women's world with self-proclaimed aspirations for women's emancipation (Sullerot 1963; Bullier 1965; Ferguson 1983; Bonvoisin and Maignien 1986; Winship 1987; Ballaster 1991; Wadia 1991; McCracken 1993; Farrell 1994; Hermes 1995; Scanlon 1995).

Through her publication, Beauvoir helped make a post-1945 "imagined sisterhood" by articulating its central tenet: the potential of the female body for political agency. Because of Beauvoir's insights, her "sisters" turned this occupation into a political agenda, which was disseminated in the feminist reviews and manifested in the collective political struggle for reproductive rights in the 1960s, 1970s, and 1980s. In addition, the popular success of women's magazines during this period, despite their central concern with commodity consumption and their focus on individual self-development, helped disseminate information on reproductive rights and sexuality. Paradoxically, then, popular women's magazines contributed to the creation of this real and imagined "sisterhood," as even the act of consuming can entail potentially counterhegemonic practices (Jenkins 1992; Storey 1996).

My study analyzes all of these types of women's writing—high feminist literature, mass cultural texts, and feminist reviews—to show how texts written by women for women who are bound together by common concerns can help propel women to become engaged politically despite their political and cultural marginalization. Women's political engagement is exemplified here by the postwar collective struggle for reproductive freedom, through which women challenged the French state to abandon its laws criminalizing abortion.

Analytical Lens and Main Theoretical Concepts

Before I proceed, a few methodological notes are in order. Given the broad scope of the issues covered here—the body, citizenship, dissent, reproductive politics—my choice of material is highly selective, and my analytical lens, a qualitative political discourse analysis of women's writings in the form of narratives, images, and symbols, may seem closer to a linguistic study than a work of political science. In this regard, I am consciously following the "Cambridge School" of political theory, exemplified by Quentin Skinner. Skinner and his followers have demonstrated that putting political thought in its social and cultural context amplifies our understanding of politics (Skinner 1978; Ball, Farr, and Hanson 1989). This study takes the next step in this direction by connecting bodily and sexual practices with everyday politics and liberatory claims for citizenship in Fifth Republic France. Furthermore, groundbreaking recent feminist political discourse analyses attest to the relevance of linking discursive patterns with (national) social policymaking following the interpretive turn in the field of political theory. Political discourse analysis demonstrates that politics is not just a struggle over what political actors want but also a struggle over *interpreting* what political actors want (Kulawik 2009).

Moreover, this study follows other recent theoretical developments in challenging traditional notions of the body, sex, and gender. My analysis of the symbolic representation of women and their bodies in a variety of different texts shows the female body to be a site of political contestation rather than a kind of "natural" biological entity. Likewise, these theories understand women's (and men's) bodies as artifacts, socially situated and acted upon by different societal forces to construct specific historical subjects—including women activists (Bourdieu 1984; Foucault 1990; Featherstone 1991; Bordo 1993; Grosz 1994; Gatens 1996; Canning 1999; Chisholm 2001). In this way, my analysis of women's liberatory discourses contributes to our understanding of women's *political activism* in democratic political systems, an issue that the field of democratic theory has only begun to systematically analyze. In short, I show how personal experiences of the body are central to women's democratic politics in modern France, which are expressed during the period of second-wave feminism in postwar France in very specific ways through rhetoric about women's equal citizenship rights to control their own bodies.

Here I should clarify some of the main concepts and terms used in this study, which should also say something about my theoretical orientation and methodology. In using the term "discourse," I do not refer to a specific text or utterance, but rather to a historically, socially, and institutionally specific structure of statements, terms, categories, and beliefs. The meaning of these structures is always contested, and the power to control their meaning usually resides in claims to (scientific) knowledge through writing, institutions (such as schools), and social relationships (such as the family). To talk about "citizenship discourse," for instance, is to acknowledge that the meaning of citizenship is in constant flux, and furthermore that the elaboration of its meaning involves conflict and power.

"Citizenship," in modern political theory, expresses the entitlement to civil and political rights held by an individual residing in a given state, and is most often associated with the democratic notion of equality under the law. But the development of citizenship rights has a long history, going back to the Greek city-states, where citizenship was bound up with the quest for social peace, or the common good, rather than individual well-being. Recent writings by feminists have focused on social contract theory to argue that the justification for keeping women out of the body politic was, and is, often made in terms of protecting the health and well-being of society from corruption and infection, a measure still observable in twentieth-century welfare politics. As a result, feminism can be understood as a protest against this unequal treatment and political exclusion (Okin 1979; Eisenstein 1981; Phillips 1987; Coole 1988, 1994; Pateman 1988; Orloff 1993; Offen 1994). Consequently, feminist theorists have argued that the concept of citizenship ought to include not just rights and obligations, which are usually associated with it, but also bodily practices, since those differ greatly between women and men. By showing that citizenship is a gendered construction and bound up with bodily practices, feminist-embodied citizenship theory significantly broadens the sense of what can be considered political in the modern state. In this study, I draw attention to how bodies themselves become sites of political struggle, that is, how the body can be used to contest or legitimate the power of the state and the meaning of citizenship (Young 1990; Schiebinger 1993; Sparks 1997; Parkins 2000, 2002). My position is that there are no bodies in a general sense, but rather (historically) specific bodies, marked by gender (and race, class, sexuality, etc.), which shows the body politic to be a gender-specific myth.

By "women's activism," I mean the political contestation undertaken by women throughout French history in general and by women's groups in the wake of the 1968 students' and workers' revolt, which ushered in the postwar women's liberation movement specifically.[1] By necessity, my concept of "women's activism" includes women's writing, as much of women's political contestation throughout French (feminist) history was undertaken through the use of writing and reading.

Finally, the concept of "sisterhood" is employed here to refer to a community or network that promotes feminist consciousness and activism. For the purposes of this study, I have defined feminism as a commitment to improving women's lives and to ending gender inequality with a specific emphasis on reproduction and the body. The concept of "sisterhood" has its theoretical roots in the nineteenth-century linkage between gender and culture, which separated women's and men's lives into distinct spheres of activity, with the added understanding that women's culture was superior to that of men. The creation of this concept goes back to the Enlightenment construction of women's function as the producer of good moral values. For the women's movements that swept through North America and Western Europe in the 1970s, the concept of "sisterhood" expressed the hope that women could leave the margins of political life to become equal citizens, yet it also raised concerns about whether women activists could speak for all women on the basis of sexual difference (Morgan 1970, 1984, 2003; Melder 1977). Arguably, French women activists found the idea of women's "sisterhood" in the theories of Simone de Beauvoir (see chap. 2) and through personal contacts and cross-border exchanges with activists and writers from other countries (Reineke 2008–2009). (As Judith Ezekiel [2002] informs us, one of the groups that made up the MLF associated "sisterhood" strictly with American-style feminism and opposed it on those grounds.)

Let me be clear: "sisterhood" as it is used in this study examines the (often uncritical) invocation of women's collective identity by women activists in their effort to contest unequal citizenship rights, which historically excluded women and their needs from public affairs.[2] My use of the concept "sisterhood" does not mean to suggest that all French women identified with it or believed that the invocation of such a collective identity would necessarily foster solidarity among women in France, whose access to women's rights, such as reproductive rights, is mitigated by differences in race, class, sexual identity, and age, among other factors. As chapter 4 will make clear, some women who engaged with the feminist struggle for reproductive freedom believed that that the politics of "sisterhood" were not radical enough to stop women's oppression. These activists argued instead that notions of "sisterhood" mirrored masculinist culture's claim that all women are the same (and different from men). Joan W. Scott (1988, 1996) has shown how this "equal-versus-difference" debate has been central to the history of French feminisms, including the period of the MLF. Important for this study, the women's activist groups that made up the MLF could agree that writing and reading constituted a distinct citizenship practice that women could use as a self-conscious vehicle for collective action (Zerilli 2005). Thus the term "sisterhood" is employed here as a heuristic device that allows us to better understand how citizens can forge a political consciousness, develop ideas, and act collectively through the everyday practice of reading and writing. Hence my theoretical emphasis rests on "imagined" sisterhood, as this is a study not of the organization known as the MLF, but of women's literary creation of a social space that promotes feminist consciousness and, potentially, political activity.

As such, an imagined "sisterhood" is a physical community or organization, like the many women's groups that made up the MLF, as well as a discursive site where feminist identities are constructed and interests are expressed. The development of the MLF during the 1970s, 1980s, and 1990s shows clearly that this imagined community or "sisterhood" entailed contending and even opposing viewpoints, as exemplified in the divergent ideological strands within the movement discussed in chapter 4.[3] However, despite or because of these existing differences, I argue that studying women activists' public writings can uncover a central focus of feminist contestations, which made the female body the main concern in the political struggle for women's rights. Clearly, I do not wish to say that because women imagined a particular "sisterhood," it was any less "real" for those who experienced this feeling of community and acted upon the consciousness and empowerment that went along with it. What these women imagined became a catalyst for a new social reality, and it gave them the political will and the tools to attain it.

Recent Scholarship

A desire to better understand how states discriminate between citizens based on their "difference" has fueled a renewed interest in democratic theory and citizenship rights studies on both sides of the Atlantic. Crucial in this development was the emergence of the so-called "new social movements" and the critical debates related to "identity politics" in the 1960s (Rowbotham 1992; Turner 1993; Tilly 1995; Martel 1999; Stevenson 2001). On this side of the Atlantic, the scholarship by Judith Shklar (1991) and John Rawls (1971) has explored the concept of distributive justice in the liberal tradition. "Deliberative democrats," such as Jürgen Habermas (1973, 1992), Seyla Benhabib (1992), and Nancy Fraser (1989), emphasize the discursive aspects of political agency, while the communitarian critique of liberal individualism, associated with the works of Alisdair MacIntyre (1981), Michael Sandel (1982), and Charles Taylor (1989), draws attention to the collective nature of citizenship practice. Another strand of democratic theory, often called "civic republican," emphasizes political judgment and autonomy for individuals in its concepts of citizenship. For scholars in this tradition, including Hannah Arendt (1972) and Benjamin Barber (1984), political participation is based on public virtue and must—by definition—exclude affairs of the private realm.

Furthermore, feminist and queer studies have contributed to our understanding of how social identities are culturally produced and reproduced, including the distinction of what counts as private and public, or outside and inside the realm of politics. Feminist studies by Pateman (1988), Vogel (1988), K. Jones (1990), Phillips (1991), Yuval-Davis (1991), Mouffe (1992), Hennessey (1993), Walby (1994), Eisenstein (1994), Frader and Rose (1996), Lister (1997), Savarsy (1997), Yuval-Davis and Werbner (1999), Patton and Caserio (2000), Siim (2000), and Yeatman (2001), but also by Charzat (1972), Delphy (1984), Fauré (1985), Fraisse (1994), Lefèbvre (2003), and others in the French context, have examined how citizenship rights are "gendered" and how women's political participation or agency can be ensured.

It is unnecessary here to undertake a review of the French feminist literature on citizenship theories, since such reviews are already plentiful (Batiot

1986; McBride Stetson 1987; Duchen 1994; Adkins and Leonard 1996; Scott 1996; Allwood 1998; Allwood and Wadia 2000, 2009; Cross 2000). In general, contributions to the study of the gendered nature of French democracy and politics fall into three distinct categories: first, publications dealing with democratic theory from a feminist point of view (see above); second, histories of French feminism and the women's liberation movement (Albistur and Armogathe 1977; Tristan and Pisan 1977; Dhavernas 1979; Kandel 1979; D. Stewart 1980; Leger 1982; Kaufmann-McCall 1983; Sarde 1983; Duchen 1986; Mossuz-Lavau 1986; Jenson 1987; Laubier 1990; Remy 1990; Delphy 1991; Duby and Perrot 1991; Picq 1993); and third, studies on the status of women in politics and the political system (Michel and Texier 1964; Mossuz-Lavau and Sineau 1983; Sineau 1988; Jenson and Sineau 1994; Latour, Houssin, and Tovar 1995; Riot-Sarcey 1995; Le Bras-Chopard and Mossuz-Lavau 1997; Bard 2001; Bard, Baudelot, and Mossuz-Lavau 2004). The celebration of the bicentennial of the French Revolution in 1989 sparked a renewed interest in feminist publications on democracy and citizenship as well as on the women's liberation movement, including some studies on the abortion issue and women's rights in postwar France (included above).

Lastly, a recent debate in France related to gender and citizenship rights evolved around the issue of "parity" (*parité*), women's right of access to elected office. The political debate ushered in the "Constitutional Reform Bill" of 1999, which sought to increase women's political representation. The many publications surrounding this movement's political goals demonstrate that, in France, the task of theorizing citizenship remains intimately linked to the history of feminist activism for women's rights (Gaspard, Servan-Schreiber, and Le Gall 1992; Fraisse 1994; Sineau 1997; Agacinski 1998). My summary of the study provided below is meant to underline once more the importance of this connection for understanding French body politics.

Summary of the Study

In order to contextualize the postwar feminist struggle for reproductive rights, my study starts with an overview in chapter 1 of the gendering of citizenship rights and women's reaction to it in early modern and modern France. While the students' and workers' revolt of May 1968 is often seen as the origin of French feminism, women's political activism actually has a long history, dating back to the Middle Ages (Albistur and Armogathe 1977). Through the centuries, women's struggle against political and cultural exclusion took on many different forms and was sometimes less successful, sometimes more, depending on the political climate and, particularly, the political system of the time (changing from monarchy to republic, to empire and back).

Crucially, as I will demonstrate, like the suffragettes and other women activists before them, the participants in the postwar women's liberation movement used the print media as a forceful tool in their political contestation. In this way, the MLF was able not only to contribute to the public discourse about women's rights, but also to build an alternative social space in which women could gather information and exchange experiences about women's issues. Importantly, the MLF made the female body a central concern in political discourse about citizenship rights, particularly in its campaign for reproductive rights.

For this reason, chapter 2 examines how one of the movement's leading theorists, Simone de Beauvoir, problematized the issue of body politics in French society. Here I am less concerned with Beauvoir's more-studied philosophical work than with her critique of postwar consumer society as reflected in her later fictional work. Read in conjunction with Beauvoir's account of women's oppression in *Le Deuxième sexe,* her representation of female corporeality offers a valuable—and hitherto unexplored—insight into feminists' attempts to foreground the importance of women's bodily experience to the debate on citizenship rights.

Chapter 3 continues to explore the postwar concept of femininity, but this time from the point of view of the mass cultural market of women's fashion and beauty magazines. Here I examine representations of the commodified female body and its use (or abuse) for commercial purposes. Not only can these magazines reproduce gender ideals, but they can also mobilize an "imagined sisterhood" bound together by common concerns, including the fight against gender inequalities. Ultimately, however, the potential of these magazines for the politics of sisterhood remains limited, as commercial media have to create an atmosphere conducive to commodity consumption, not political and social transformation.

Lauren Berlant's valuable study on the conflation of politics and consumerism informs my analysis of popular magazines' (a)political agenda in this chapter and throughout this study. Berlant shows how popular magazines participate in the construction of gendered desires for freedom, liberation, and community, and how these desires become channeled into commodity consumption, including the commodification of women's bodies, that at times undermines the political mobilization of women for gender equality (Berlant 1997). It is precisely this lack of women's bodily agency that the women's liberation movement contested in its focus on the female body to demand reproductive rights.

Thus, the last chapter examines the small-scale feminist reviews published by the women's liberation movement during the 1970s and 1980s, which were used to fight women's political and cultural exclusion. I argue that these publications succeeded in constructing an alternative social space for women outside of consumer ideology. As an avenue for political dissent, the reviews not only connected women with one another through the medium of writing, but also contributed to making a collective feminist identity in postwar France. In this way, the women's liberation movement ultimately challenged the political system and contributed to making abortion one of the most salient political issues in postwar French politics.

While the MLF no longer exists in France, many feminists will acknowledge the continuing existence of specific feminist groups and projects. As we have seen, one such feminist project is the parity movement for women's right of access to elected office in France. The parity movement developed in the early 1990s out of a number of challenges to the political system based on group rights. In contrast to the earlier feminist campaigns for women's rights—those for the right to vote and the right to reproductive freedom—this political campaign endeavored to show that "women" were neither the same as nor different from "men," and that women and men therefore deserved equal political representation. Members of the parity project argued that the basis of republican citizenship, namely, abstract individualism, had to include, not exclude, sex in order to ensure real equality. The parity movement's efforts culminated in a new electoral law. A constitutional amendment, it requires that half of all candidates participating in national, regional, and municipal elections for political office be women (Scott 2005, 2, 4).

Like earlier feminist movements, the parity movement illustrates how women's exclusion from political representation based on a disembodied concept of citizenship sparked very specific political strategies to rectify this exclusion. While the political strategies developed by women's rights activists have differed throughout history, feminist activists understood that in France, questions of embodiment make women rally around political causes. In order to contextualize feminist responses to gendered citizenship rights, the first chapter will provide some important background information for understanding French body politics.

Beauvoir and Her Sisters

1 The Body, Writing, and Citizenship Rights

BEFORE I TURN TO ANALYZING how three specific types of women's writing—high feminist literature (chap. 2), popular women's magazines (chap. 3), and feminist reviews (chap. 4)—helped create an alternative social space for women to gather information and exchange experiences about female sexuality and reproductive rights in postwar France, this chapter will provide important historical and contextual background information. This information will help in understanding how the political exclusion of women based on a disembodied concept of citizenship sparked very specific political strategies by women as they attempted to rectify this exclusion. As I hope to show in the following chapters, one such strategy was the use of reading and writing. It allowed women to straddle the borders of private and public life and enabled them to turn an ordinary social practice into potentially political practices.

Joan W. Scott (2005) has identified three broad yet specific moments in French history when questions of embodiment made women rally for equal citizenship rights: the campaign for women's right to vote in the nineteenth century; the campaign for reproductive rights in the 1960s, 1970s, and 1980s; and the campaign for women's right to access to elected office (*parité*) in the 1990s. My study focuses on the second of those campaigns. After women acquired the right to vote, activists in the 1960s, 1970s, and 1980s reacted to persisting political and social inequalities, including the restrictive abortion law that denied women the right to control their own bodies. During this period, I argue, activists rediscovered women's writing as a forceful tool for fostering a political consciousness among women and potentially creating a real collective agency. To this end, they made the female body a central political locus of the feminist campaign for reproductive rights. However, at the same time that women's writing aimed to construct a shared female identity and political consciousness that centered on female bodily experiences—exemplified, for instance, in women's writing about their experiences with sexuality, pregnancy, and motherhood—postwar consumer culture constructed the female body as an object of consumer desire rather than as a subject of individual citizenship rights. This peculiar historical context, I suggest, created distinctive challenges for the postwar women's liberation movement, which produced at times ambiguous results.

In what follows, I shall provide essential background information on citizenship rights discourses and the body in French history in order to contextualize my subsequent analysis of women's writing in postwar society. For this purpose, I have divided this chapter into three distinct sections. The first section examines the specific concepts of citizenship rights developed in early modern and modern France and how those concepts impacted women's social and political status. It also considers the first "feminist" responses to the gendering of citizenship rights following the French Revolution. The second section then offers contextual and background information on the development of French feminism in the nineteenth century, which centered on the campaign for the right to vote. The third section contextualizes the feminist campaign for reproductive freedom of the twentieth century, which began in the 1960s.

Gendered Concepts of Citizenship Rights in Early Modern and Modern France

In France, as historians inform us, the gendering of public affairs and citizenship rights mirrors a deep-seated fear of women's influence on political life. This fear goes back to the Salic law of the Middle Ages, which excluded female offspring from inheriting rights to the throne. In early modern France, as a result, "political" women were demonized, and political authority was gendered so as to exclude women from public life (Hanley and Denizard 1994).[1] For example, recent scholarship examining public charges made against perhaps the most famous political woman in early modern France, Queen Marie-Antoinette, demonstrates how her critics used sexual stereotypes, such as women's supposedly insatiable sexual and economic appetite, to portray her as a political threat to the social order. In this case, the royal account books in which the queen's expenditures on fashion and jewelry were recorded were later used to indict her for causing the bankruptcy of the French state and, ultimately, the downfall of the monarchy. By extension, critics used her case to justify the exclusion of all women from public life and citizenship in the new republic (J. Jones 1996; Marso 2006, chap. 2). I suggest that this construal of the queen's spending habits as a political threat to French society illustrates the processes involved in gendering early modern and modern French political culture and citizenship rights, which relegated women to secondary citizens.

Concepts of citizenship in early modern and modern France were grounded philosophically in seventeenth- and eighteenth-century social contract theories dating back to the early modern natural law theories of Hugo Grotius, Thomas Hobbes, Benedict de Spinoza, and John Locke, which emphasized individual rights and entitlement. Based on the notion of sovereign power, social contract theories posit that individuals enter into contracts with one another in order to create a political authority (called the state), which protects life and property and secures individual liberties. In return, individuals, now called citizens, are granted political and civil (and later social) rights by this authority that governs their lives.

According to one prominent social contract theorist, Jean-Jacques Rousseau (1712–78), women's civic role was to be mothers and educators of future (male) citizens, not to meddle in public affairs. In his *Social Contract* (1762), Rousseau called upon women to govern the family and household and to raise the next generation of virtuous citizens (Reynolds 1987; Marso 1999). He wrote: "Happy are we, so long as your chaste influence, solely exercised within the limits of conjugal union, is exerted only for the glory of the State and the happiness of the public. . . . It is your task to perpetuate, by your insinuating influence and your innocent and amiable rule, a respect for the laws of the State, and harmony among the citizens" ([1762] 1920, 166). Soon, the events of the Revolution of 1789 revealed that this new citizenry demanded individuality and economic well-being as much as civic participation. Earlier, the political theories of Charles de Secondat, Baron de la Brède et de Montesquieu (1698–1755), stressed the importance of private activities, including the market and family affairs, as a source of individual happiness (Montesquieu 1874). In this classic liberal view, citizenship is based on the protection of individual rights (and possessions) by the state rather than on the civic virtues of its citizens (Macpherson 1962). Benjamin Constant ([1818] 1980) aptly described this changed understanding of citizenship in his *Essai sur la liberté des anciens comparée à celle des modernes* as one of not "political" but "private" individuals endowed with individual freedoms.

The sweeping political changes brought about by the Revolution, which sought to implement these new and indeed radical ideas, did not extend to women. Even propertied women were now barred from political participation (voting). In this way, women were denied active citizenship. Legislators grouped them together with children and minors to be governed by protective laws, which they had no power to change (McBride Stetson 1987). As Geneviève Fraisse and Scott show in their detailed studies on the birth of modern French democracy, the republican concept of citizenship was technically gender neutral as it de facto included women and men, but the universal concept of individual rights on which it rested was gendered from the beginning. As Scott explains, "Ideological/political systems such as French republicanism work by endorsing the notion that coherence is a requirement for social organization and then by presenting themselves as fulfilling the requirements for coherence. . . . Thus, the production of 'sexual difference' was a way of achieving the otherwise inconsistent exclusion of women from the categories of individual and citizen" (1996, 11–12).

Social commentators defended this political exclusion, emphasizing women's innate weakness and need of male protection. At the same time, they stressed women's purported moral superiority over men to justify women's and men's different status. Women's political marginalization was nowhere more evident than in a 1793 decree outlawing all women's groups and a 1795 decree denying women the right to assembly (Rogers 1984, 43). As Fraisse explains in her study, "Women's rights were not inadvertently overlooked, but were denied out of necessity" (1994, xv), because women were perceived to be a source of division in the new republic. As Harriet B. Applewhite and Darline Gay Levy state, active citizenship was to be reserved for a new elite of white, moneyed men, as "women were legislated out of the political nation, with sex-based arguments thrown in to rationalize the application of a brutal power politics" (1984, 77).

Applewhite and Levy's studies are part of a growing area of new and important research in French history focusing on the role of women in the French Revolution. These studies offer new insights into women's political mobilization and actual involvement in political radicalization and street riots leading up to and during the Revolution.[2] Building on these discoveries, Carla Hesse (2002) has shown that the revolutionary upheaval enabled an increasing number of women to participate in public discourses about citizenship rights through the act of writing. Although the number of women who could read and write remained limited to a small elite, the voice that women gained through the writing of essays and novels turned an otherwise innocent activity into a *political* practice of contestation, or what Holloway Sparks has called "citizenship dissent" (1997, 75).[3] In her pathbreaking study *The Other Enlightenment,* Hesse claims that "the French Revolution opened up the unprecedented opportunity for women . . . to debate the appropriate place for women within a democratic society" (2002, 5).

What women writers lacked, however, was a *collective* basis for promoting women's concerns. During the eighteenth century, *salonnières,* upper-class women who held regular meetings in their homes so that local intellectuals and aristocrats could converse about important topics and listen to public readings (including those of women), constituted a very small group of privileged women. Susan P. Conner and others (Goodman 1994; Roche 1998; Kale 2004) have argued that eighteenth-century *salonnières*

> should not be discussed in studies of political women. Their inclusion has actually been a case of mistaking visibility with political power. Scarcely on the periphery of politics, *salonnières* were prominent not in politics but in social circles as inheritors of the tradition of the *précieuses* of the previous century. Like their predecessors, they continued to discuss controversial topics and to surround themselves with men of learning. Some continued to revolt against contemporary marriage customs; some studied literature that promoted equality between the sexes, although not particularly as feminists; and some wrote pamphlets and books that frequently contained political overtones. . . . But the *salonnières* and writers did not step beyond their salons and discussions. (Conner 1984, 50)

As for the French Revolution, Jane Abray attributes the "almost total failure of revolutionary feminism" after 1789 to the lack of collective action due in part to the suppression of women's clubs as early as 1793 (1975, 58). If there was no women's revolution following the Great Revolution, however, "women's writing flourished once [the old] regime fell" (Hesse 2002, 37), enabling women's participation in literature and public discourse through the commercialization of cultural life. In short, one way of reading the events of the Revolution is to acknowledge the significance for the emergence of women's political activity of a developing public culture, or sphere—particularly through public print media—that remains important today.

Among the types of writings that thrived in what Jürgen Habermas has called the "bourgeois public sphere" (1992, 89) are the three genres examined in this study: high literature, popular magazines, and political reviews. Women used all three new literary spaces to exchange experiences and opinions, including opinions on political matters. In this way, they turned ordinary social practices such as reading and writing into acts of political contestation and, potentially, agency.

Perhaps the most notorious example of women's participation in public political discourse during the Revolution, which was still very much limited to the privileged women of the upper class, was Olympe de Gouges's *Declaration of the Rights of Woman* (*Déclaration des droits de la femme et de la citoyenne*), addressed to the National Assembly in 1791. Modeled on the Assembly's *Declaration of the Rights of Man and Citizen* (*Déclaration des droits de l'homme et du citoyen*) from 1789, this political tract (Gouges [1791] 1979) urged the Assembly not to forget about women's equality. It should be noted here that already prior to the Revolution, women had petitioned the king seeking ameliorations in women's education and work conditions. Like Gouges, these women had hoped that their voices would be heard and that their political claims could be included in postrevolutionary reforms. Likewise, the Marquis de Condorcet and a few other men had argued for women's political rights as early as 1790 (Landes 1988; Hunt 1996, 60–63). Yet, like Marie-Antoinette, Gouges ended up on the guillotine in 1793 before any of her political demands could be considered. Interestingly, for her actions Gouges was charged with "crimes of the pen" against the government, following an earlier practice in accordance with which challenging writers and their works were considered a civic menace. As Joan DeJean (1991) informs us in her insightful study on the origins of the modern novel in France, women's writings, which started in France as early as the 1660s as a vehicle for feminist ideas, posed a particular political challenge and thus a threat to civic stability. She reports on another such female writer, Anne Louise Germaine de Staël-Holstein, or Madame de Staël, who was exiled from Paris after the Revolution for her literary work (8).

Despite, or because of, these setbacks, the bourgeois public sphere offered women a medium for challenging the idea of republican citizenship, which had promised universal equality but had limited it to a certain—male—type of individual who stood in for the universal model on which it claimed to rest. As French historians have explained, the gendering of French public culture offered feminists an opportunity to claim political rights for women as they revealed the "paradox" of republican citizenship (Scott 1996, 3). As Scott explains, when early feminists attempted to speak on behalf of women as a group, they forged their political claims around the very same paradox that they wanted to defeat. In this instance, they used the idea of republican motherhood to claim political rights for women based on their reproductive functions, namely, their fundamental difference from men (Hunt 1994; Scott

1996; Foley 2004). Scott writes: "Feminism was a protest against women's political exclusion; its goal was to eliminate 'sexual difference' in politics, but it had to make its claims on behalf of 'women' (who were discursively produced through 'sexual difference'). To the extent that it acted for 'women,' feminism produced the 'sexual difference' it sought to eliminate. This paradox—the need both to accept *and* to refuse 'sexual difference'—was the constitutive condition of feminism as a political movement throughout its long history" (1996, 3–4).

Important for this study, while feminist claims for women's political rights fought the contradictory model of universal citizenship, they drew attention to women's sexed body and its political significance: women's exclusion from politics and public affairs (Scott 2005). Although scholars debate whether women's exclusion from the public sphere was intrinsic to the masculinist republican model or a constantly renegotiated facet of republican public culture, I want to emphasize how feminist oppositional discourses made the female body a focus in the struggle against women's political marginalization, which was later expressed in women's claim to the right to control their own bodies (Landes 1988; Hesse 2002). There are a number of examples of women's rights activists in France and elsewhere who made a woman's right to bodily self-determination the focus of their political struggle for equal citizenship rights. These include the feminist campaigns for free and legal abortion, which popularized the slogan "Our bellies belong to us" and made public the confessions of hundreds of women who had had illegal abortions. These protest campaigns allowed feminists to break the silence of women who had experienced unwanted pregnancies and/or clandestine abortions, and to demonstrate to the larger public the absurdity of existing repressive abortion laws that denied women equal rights (Reineke 2008–2009).

Women's claim to the right to control their own bodies originates in the liberal concepts of individual freedom and autonomy discussed above. Feminists appropriated the liberal view to argue that true individual autonomy is possible only if one achieves control over one's own body. Since women's bodies differ from men's in that they are potentially engaged in the reproduction of the human species, reproductive freedom becomes the litmus test for how the state extends liberal citizenship rights (Batiot 1986; Petchesky 1995). In France, a person's right to control his body is codified in the *Code civil* (or *Code Napoléon*), dating back to 1804, and is today an integral part of article 16 of the Civil Code governing a citizen's right to physical integrity.[4]

However, women remained excluded from equal citizenship rights on the basis of their bodily difference from men, because, as Scott explains, "sexual difference, in the person of the woman, was not included in the list of traits that could be abstracted for purposes of citizenship. Women's exclusion was not just about eliminating women's influence. It also served a major symbolic function as a reminder of the existence of irreducible difference—unresolvable antagonism within the national body, which posed a threat to the abstraction and thus the very existence of national unity" (2005, 16).

Unsurprisingly, women responded strongly to their continued political exclusion based on a concept of abstract universalism that discriminated against women as the embodiment of (sexual) difference (Pateman 1988; Offen 1994, 2003). In fact, a plethora of (male) literature directed toward silencing women, such as conduct books and advice manuals, "may actually represent a highly unsuccessful effort to dam a flow of female energy and activity that could be stopped only by systematic, sustained intervention" (Offen 2003, 739; see also Jordanova 1982; Veauvy and Pisano 1997).

Despite these roadblocks, women's political activism started to take off in the nineteenth century with the rise of Saint-Simonian socialism and the Revolution of 1848 leading to the establishment of the Second Republic (1848–51). In fact, the first autonomous women's movement evolved out of the Saint-Simonian movement in the early 1830s. Flora Tristan, Jeanne Deroin, and Pauline Roland remain most strongly associated with this era, at the same time that the first feminist newspapers and journals tried to link the plight of the working class with the struggle for women's rights (McMillan 1981, 79; Moses 1984, chaps. 3 and 4). Tristan, for instance, an active leader of the French working-class movement, emphasized women's right to work for a remunerative wage as well as divorce laws. Her work was an uphill struggle, however, because it was not until 1848 that the Provisional Government of the Second Republic recognized men's right to work after the institution of "universal" male suffrage (Moses 1984, 102, 110).

Deroin took up where Tristan had left off. In particular, she fought for women's right to work and to vote. Deroin's strategy was to point out an apparent tension in the new constitution. She argued that because women had duties and obligations that were stated in the constitution, such as caring for husband, family, and children, they must be considered citizens. With this argument, Deroin, like other nineteenth-century feminists, managed to appropriate the concept of republican motherhood for her own political ends (Scott 1996, 67–70; Cova 1997). As Claire Goldberg Moses explains, "Defining woman as mother was not, of course, a new idea. . . . In the nineteenth century, it was embellished by female educational writers . . . to buttress their arguments that women should be better educated. Exalting women's role as mother was not even new to feminists. . . . Now, however, [it] became the linchpin of the feminist rationale for sexual equality" (1984, 133).

Following the victory of the conservative forces in the April 1848 parliamentary elections, however, feminist voices were soon silenced, and women's print media and women's clubs were once again suppressed. As before, political authorities were able to turn women's political activism into a threat to the social order, by depicting women as man-haters and enemies of the family because of feminists' association with libertarian sexual theories and the campaign for the reintroduction of divorce. In the 1850s, with the establishment of the imperial government of Napoléon III, or the Second Empire, "feminism" ceased to exist altogether as women were relegated to the domestic sphere. Paradoxically, it was during this period in French history that the modern feminist movement was born. Its foundations were laid by two political activists, Léon Richter and Maria Deraismes, who also published the longest-lived liberal feminist newspaper, *Le Droit des femmes* (McMillan 1981, 81).

But it was not until the events of the Paris Commune of 1871 and the establishment of the Third Republic (1871–1940) following the Franco-Prussian War that the feminist movement really took off. Germany had declared war on France in July 1870 and defeated it in only two months. In the ensuing political vacuum, republicans announced the erection of the Third Republic in Versailles. The so-called Paris Commune was established as a counter-government to the Versailles government after French army troops botched a raid in Paris. From the beginning, women were actively involved in the Commune; some even fought on the barricades. However, when large parts of Paris were burned down during the final week of the Commune, women were accused of starting the fires. These women were referred to in the press as *pétroleuses* ("women incendiaries"). As we know today, the *pétroleuses* were "almost entirely a figment of the government's and the conservative press's imagination" (Gullickson 1992, 136), as the regime tried to find a scapegoat for the unfortunate turn of events. The image of the *pétroleuse,* of course, fits the description of the unruly woman who was out to destroy French society and culture, once again turning women's political activism into a threat to the social order.

After the experiences with the socialist Commune, the feminist movement turned liberal and returned to the programs of Deraismes and Richter. Therefore, for the election campaign to a new National Assembly in 1871, the movement focused on women's political rights, specifically women's suffrage (Klejman and Rochefort 1984; Moses 1984, 193–94).

The Campaign for Women's Right to Vote

Two organizations were instrumental in winning women the right to vote: first, the already existing Association pour le droit des femmes (Association for the Rights of Women), and second, the newly founded Ligue française pour le droit des femmes (French Women's Rights League). But it was the radical activist Hubertine Auclert who fervently advanced the issue of women's suffrage. Her argument that only through the acquisition of political rights would women gain significant social and civil rights was extreme for her times, as even the Commune had been able to introduce only moderate reforms for the status of women. Auclert proclaimed: "A change in the political condition of society would not help the destiny of women. . . . A change in the social and economic order would not free women; for even though every day the economic question may be resolved for a small number of women, their position would be the same the following day as it was the previous day. In France, women who are millionaires are subject to the same tyrannical laws as poor women" (Moses 1984, 215).

To underline her point, in 1881 Auclert, together with her husband and another editor, founded the weekly newspaper *La Citoyenne* (Woman Citizen). It was also Auclert who first spoke of "feminism" (*féminisme*) in the late 1890s, to reflect the importance of political rights for women's emancipation (see "Introduction," n. 1). (Following Auclert's example, Marguerite Durand launched the first feminist daily newspaper, *La Fronde* [The Sling], in 1897.)

To understand what was holding women's enfranchisement back at this particular moment in French history, we must look at the ideological polarization within the National Assembly, which was split between republicans and monarchists. Republicans hesitated to give women the vote out of fear that they would then support the (Catholic) monarchists, who opposed republicanism as a political system. As it was, the Catholic Church had a large impact on girls' and women's lives and belief systems, as it provided education for girls and functioned as a gathering place for women.[5] Consequently, conservatives from both camps wanted to postpone the suffrage question until the new republic was more securely established. Advocates of women's suffrage argued that throughout French history, women had been able to vote, for instance when voting was tied to landed property qualifications and not to "individual rights." Opponents insisted that the law stipulated that "in order to be an elector, one must be a citizen and that the citizen is the Frenchman who has full political and civil rights" (Offen 1994, 156–57). In other words, according to the circular reasoning behind this argument, because women have neither civil nor political rights and are thus not citizens, they cannot vote.

This apparent inequality of women and men before the law did, however, create an outburst of public debate over the "woman question" and fostered some social reforms geared toward women. But as historians of the Third Republic inform us, few of the numerous civil and economic reforms advocated by and for women were realized, as (male) legislators were more concerned about protecting—and controlling—women (Klejman and Rochefort 1989; Bard 1995). The desire to control women's behavior was particularly striking in connection with fertility control. During the second half of the nineteenth century, social commentators and politicians obsessed over the causes and meaning of a falling birthrate, fearing a weakened French nation in comparison to a belligerent Germany. Specifically, these nationalistic sentiments supported pronatalist policies that were meant to counter the use of (female) contraceptives, as women, not men, had been blamed for a falling fertility rate.[6]

As Danielle Hassou (1997) has shown in her study on French legislation regarding contraception and abortion, French pronatalist history goes back to the nineteenth century, when France experienced a decline in its national birthrate. The drop was partly caused by a sharp increase in urbanization, industrialization, and the ensuing poverty of large segments of the population during the eighteenth century. As Hassou explains, French women and men traditionally restricted their fertility on a voluntary basis, following the upper-class model of limiting the number of children in order to keep the inheritance from being broken up. During the Industrial Revolution, this "neo-Malthusian" behavior became even more popular as the idea of social mobility inspired many working-class families to limit childbearing to one or two children and to provide well for them in the hope for a better life. Originally, Thomas Malthus (1766–1834), an English pastor and economist who argued that an impending overpopulation would cause widespread socioeconomic misery due to a lack of food, had directed his ideas of sexual self-restraint toward men rather than women. Malthus proposed a number of moral measures to stop citizens from having too many children, including delaying marriage, forgoing sex outside marriage, and practicing sexual abstinence. The Malthusian League, which formed in England in 1877, followed his ideas but replaced sexual abstinence with the use of contraception and safe abortions (Ruhl 2002, 648).

However, just as a neo-Malthusian movement emerged in France at the end of the nineteenth century, it was countered by pronatalist state policies embodied in repressive family and health laws (Accampo, Fuchs, and Stewart 1995; Cova 1997; Accampo 2003, 2006). This was especially true for the decades following the French defeat in the Franco-Prussian War of 1870–71, which pitted a large and threatening German population and army against a diminishing French one. In the twentieth century, the powerful Catholic Church and the humiliating defeat in World War II would reinforce the French state's pronatalist policies for a while. As we shall see, in its most conservative form, during the Occupation and the Vichy regime, a strong nationalist and racist ideology backed these policies, and politicians painted the French neo-Malthusians as treasonous.

But let us return to the issue of women's voting rights. By the time the suffrage question finally arrived on the political agenda of the National Assembly in 1900, it had become intertwined with a broader, seemingly more pressing question: the issue of electoral reform for proportional representation. Yet even feminists' strategies to win the vote for women by emphasizing women's difference as "citizen-mothers," in order to appeal to legislators' desire to protect maternity and infancy, failed once again. Even worse, with the beginning of World War I in 1914, the question of women's suffrage disappeared from French politics altogether, pushing political rights, but not gender issues, off the political agenda (Frader 2008; Stanley 2008). As Mary Louise Roberts aptly explains, gender relations continued to preoccupy lawmakers in the interwar period and beyond: "Throughout the nineteenth century, debates about female identity and women's role gained broad significance. Debates concerning women played a crucial part in the public discussion of other matters important to social, political, and economic life—the problems of industrialization and urbanization, and the construction of the welfare state, to name a few. The postwar debate on women simply continued a decades-long pattern in which gender issues were at the forefront of French political, social, and literary discourse" (1994, 8).

In the interwar period, then, three competing images of female identity stood side by side: the "modern woman," who represented change from earlier gender ideals; the "mother," who represented continuity and tradition and who served the state through sacrificing her body in birth; and the "single woman," who oscillated between the other two, but more generally reflected postwar demographic concerns over France's birthrate in the absence of marriageable men. The first of the three images, the "modern woman," was a true product of the war, as it allowed women, for the first time in French history, to work and live independently and to enjoy a first glimpse of female sexual freedom. However, when more and more wives of soldiers were accused of sexual infidelity while their husbands were away, this (perceived or real) gender transgression caused alarm in French society, not least because of paternity questions. The postwar cultural icon of the "mother," by contrast, symbolized physical and moral suffering and reflected state natalist discourse.

Echoing these population concerns, Parliament introduced a bill in 1920 criminalizing the advertising and use of contraceptives and abortion. Interestingly, the law did not forbid the use of condoms and consequently did nothing to raise the French birthrate. Critics of the law thus argued that its purpose was simply "to bring women's sexual practices under legislative control [by] attacking abortion and female forms of contraception" (Roberts 1994, 96). Three years later, the law of March 27, 1923, completed this undertaking by repressing abortion itself. What is most striking about these laws is that they regarded abortion as an infraction against the state, putting population concerns above even moral considerations, and thereby using women instrumentally for French pronatalist policies.

The social activist Nelly Roussel, who later organized the first family planning programs in France, promptly attacked the pronatalist propaganda: "No matter how stupid the people are . . . you would nevertheless be hard pressed to get them to admit that in the state of economic, financial and psychological 'collapse' in which we find ourselves . . ., and at a time when our shaken, exhausted race has hardly begun its convalescence after the terrible shock [of the war], that a multiplication of births would be a benefit for the country!" (Roberts 1994, 118). In Roussel's and other feminists' opinion, World War I had not "liberated" women, despite the appearance of the modern childless young woman who wanted to take advantage of the promises of the emerging postwar consumer society. Rather, the postwar push for a technocratic society in the hands of a right-wing government elite, together with the rise of consumer society, culminated in the 1940s in women's debasement under the Vichy regime. As a political ally of Nazi Germany, Vichy implemented policies toward women that combined a belief in traditional domesticity with a modernized socioeconomic order, which provided maternity allowances and other benefits to mothers (Roberts 1994, 217). Most appalling, however, was the regime's "human engineering" program, which turned women into reproductive machines. Not surprisingly, it was the Vichy regime that introduced the death penalty for abortionists and women seeking abortions. (The last woman guillotined by the French state for practicing abortion died in 1943.)

Following World War II, women were enfranchised in 1944. But as Claire Duchen shows in her study of women's rights in postwar France, when Charles de Gaulle finally decreed women's right to vote, he presented this right as "continuing a feminine tradition of duty and thinking of others" (Duchen 1994, 35). And because enfranchisement came about by decree from the president and not through the National Assembly, the legislative body, many commentators have described it as a "paternal gift" to women rather than their legal entitlement (Offen 1994, 161). In the meantime, abortion laws returned to their pre-Vichy status, but they still prohibited contraception, birth control advice, and abortion, and they still threatened women with imprisonment (Allison 1994). A continued concern about depopulation supported these strict measures and coalesced in official pronatalist state policies, which legislated expansive family and maternity benefits, including state-supported maternity allowances; free maternity, prenatal, delivery, and postpartum care; and birth premiums. In many cases, the government adopted prenatal allowances, which covered a mother's expenses during pregnancy, to discourage abortions. In an attempt to control demographic patterns, the French government explicitly tried to regulate private sexuality, and the primary targets were women (Jenson 1986; Accampo, Fuchs, and Stewart 1995; Mossuz-Lavau 1999).

In the 1960s, however, the pronatalist agenda began to create conflicts for the many women who believed it was in their self-interest to control their own fertility. At this time, more and more women were graduating from institutions of postsecondary education, and they began to enter professions that had previously been reserved for men. Once in these careers, they found it important to be able to plan and control their pregnancies (Ruhl 2002). At this time of spectacular economic recovery, the hard-line pronatalist attitudes changed, after France experienced a rise in its birthrate and could even boast its own "baby boom" in the 1950s and 1960s. Surprisingly, perhaps, neo-Malthusianism experienced a revival in the 1950s, and in 1956 activists created the Mouvement français pour le planning familial (MFPF), which, alongside the women's liberation movement and the radical doctors' and health workers' organization the Groupe information santé (GIS), pushed for free and legal access to contraception and abortion and thereby shifted the debate about fertility from demographic concerns to women's reproductive rights (Roberts 1994; Hassou 1997). (The role of the GIS as a catalyst in the national abortion debate remains less studied but deserves greater attention. As we will see in chapter 4, while some doctors supported the feminist campaign for women's rights, their primary concern was changing the French health system, which they deemed inadequate and dangerous to patients because it forced clandestine abortions upon women [GIS 1974; Garcia 2005; Engeli 2009].)

Recent analyses have superbly told the political story of the making of the French abortion law, including the role of the women's liberation movement (Maillard 1974; Ferrand and Jaspard 1987; Jenson 1987; Allison 1994). Thus I shall only briefly recount those elements which are most important for my study.

The Campaign for Women's Right to Reproductive Freedom

The story of the making of the French law to decriminalize abortion begins in July 1970, when a conservative deputy of the National Assembly introduced a bill (the Peyret Proposition) that would legalize "therapeutic" abortions for both medical and nonmedical reasons. (In France, public health terminology distinguishes between "therapeutic" and "elective" abortions, which are initiated by personal choice rather than for medical or socioeconomic reasons.) The Peyret initiative no doubt followed the 1967 law that decriminalized the sale and use of contraception, and also mirrored the larger discussion of sexual politics that followed the 1968 revolt. Though the proposal failed, it made abortion, like contraception before it, an important political issue.

Following this legislative proposal, activists tried to raise public consciousness about abortion and thereby pressure legislators to change the existing laws. There were four primary media events that served to increase public awareness about the issue (see chap. 4). In August 1970, nine women trespassed at the Tomb of the Unknown Soldier in Paris, where they laid a wreath in memory of the soldier's unknown wife. These women, whom the media referred to as "the women's liberation movement," wanted to draw public attention to the persisting sexual and political inequalities in Fifth Republic France by targeting reproductive rights. In April 1971, the popular news magazine *Le Nouvel Observateur* published a "manifesto" by 343 women, all of whom confessed to having had an illegal abortion (MLF 1971).[7] They included prominent activists and public figures such as Simone de Beauvoir, who was instrumental in composing the statement (Tristan and Pisan 1977, 63–69). It may have been this manifesto that made the women's liberation movement public. Two months later, in June 1971, the medical profession became involved when 600 doctors published an open letter in which they confessed to having performed illegal abortions. Taken together, these two manifestos pointed to the gap between existing law and social reality.

Finally, in October–November 1972, abortion became front-page news when a mother and three other women were prosecuted under the 1920 law in the Court of Bobigny for having allegedly arranged and subsequently performed an abortion on a minor. At the center of the so-called Bobigny trial ("le procès de Bobigny") was sixteen-year-old Marie-Claire Chevalier, who had become pregnant by her high school boyfriend. Her mother had turned for help to the organization Choisir la cause des femmes, which was founded in 1971 by four prominent individuals (the lawyer Gisèle Halimi, the writer Christiane Rochefort, the academic Jean Rostand, and the philosopher Simone de Beauvoir) to offer free legal advice to women who were accused of breaking the abortion law. Halimi agreed to defend the four women in the Bobigny case, and her strategy paid off: she successfully argued that a large number of women were put at risk each year in France by having to obtain unsafe illegal abortions. The court suspended the case against the girl and found the women guilty, but fined them only a nominal fee that "really indicated victory" (Association Choisir 1975; Duchen 1986, 53).

Although the "Manifesto of the 343," which Halimi, Beauvoir, and Rochefort had signed, referred to "one million" French women who underwent illegal abortions each year, that estimate was obviously an exaggeration; the number of undeclared cases would have been difficult for the activists to determine, and many women went abroad for the procedure. The actual number of illegal abortions prior to decriminalization was about 120,000 a year. (Maternal deaths from abortion in France averaged about 40 to 50 per year from 1952 to 1972 and started to decline only when women began to resist non–medically assisted abortion practices as these became a concern for doctors and the wider public in the early 1970s [Dumont and Legrand 1981; Dumont 2002; Bajos et al. 2004; MFPF 2005].)[8]

The infamous "Bobigny affair" demonstrated the huge gap that existed in France between the law as it stood then and people's adherence to it. Quickly, the widely publicized trial created a demand for information about abortion, and it became a rallying point for public opinion. By this time, polls suggested that two thirds of French people supported some liberalization of the existing abortion law (Allison 1994, 228).

As abortion became a hot-button issue, traditional political parties and interest groups entered the fray. In 1972, for example, the Communist Party sponsored an abortion bill in Parliament, and the Socialist Party followed suit in 1973. In the meantime, more doctors published open manifestos in the prominent newspapers *Le Monde* and *Le Nouvel Observateur,* declaring that they too had performed illegal abortions. Following a period of intense activity by lobbyists from both sides, including large protest marches organized by the MLF in Paris in 1971, 1973, and 1974 that were attended by thousands of people, a legislative proposal was drawn up by the conservative prime minister, Pierre Messmer, and the health minister, Michel Poniatowski. This plan sought to legalize abortion in cases of rape, incest, and serious malformation of the child, or when women would otherwise experience physical, mental, or psychological distress (Maillard 1974).

Valéry Giscard d'Estaing, the center-right candidate who won the presidential election in 1974, supported the Messmer-Poniatowski bill. A more liberal abortion bill was circulated by his Socialist opponent, François Mitterand, but the measure failed to capture the female electorate. In November 1974, Giscard d'Estaing's newly appointed health minister, Simone Veil, led the first parliamentary debate on the new abortion law. After a heated debate, the bill was approved 284 to 189 by an alliance of left and centrist deputies; it was written into law on January 17, 1975 (Mossuz-Lavau 1986; Allison 1994; Jenson and Sineau 1994). Despite this success, the new law had considerable limits: it was valid for only five years, and abortion was legal only for women in distress, and only up to the tenth week of pregnancy. The text of the law read: "Article 1: The law guarantees respect for all humans from the beginning of life. . . . Article 4, Section I: A pregnant woman in a situation of distress may demand an abortion from a doctor. The abortion can only take place before the end of the tenth week of pregnancy. . . . A woman who demands an abortion . . . must undergo counseling" at an appropriate counseling center (Loi no. 75–17).[9]

The "Veil law," as it became known, encompassed three principles: first, women's responsibility for reproduction ("choice"); second, the dissuasion of women from having abortions through mandatory counseling; and third, the reinstatement of the state as the final authority over reproductive issues. The third element was particularly important to the government, because the 1920 and 1923 laws had not been upheld by doctors and patients, effectively undermining the state's authority (Picq 1993, 167). The government thus celebrated the new abortion law as a turning point in French sexual politics by claiming that it had shifted the focus away from sexual morality. As one woman activist explained: "In the place of sexual morality, which was to guarantee chastity through the interdiction of abortion, it is the responsibility over procreation that is now declared" (ibid., 170).

For the MLF, the new abortion law did not go far enough, as it restricted abortions up to the tenth gestational week; discriminated against minors and foreign women, who were excluded from its coverage; and reinforced class distinctions among women, as abortions were still not reimbursed by social security (*sécurité sociale*). Most importantly, the new law left the decision regarding abortion in the hands of the (male) medical establishment, as it required women to undergo medical and social counseling prior to having the procedure. In their plea to leave to women the decision for or against an abortion, the MLF argued: "For the M.L.F., abortion concerns first of all women. It is an experience, an anguish, a pain for all women, even if it is not the same for all women depending on their social standing. It is a threat that weighs on the body, a collective condemnation of which they [women] need to free themselves" (Picq 1993, 159).

Quite simply, the new regulation reflected lawmakers' refusal to upset conservative and Catholic forces and thus upheld the sanctity of (unborn) life over women's choice. Lawmakers justified the new law by saying that it protected women from the dangers of clandestine abortions. It did not, however, recognize a woman's right to control her own body. This latter point, of course, was becoming central to the feminist campaign against abortion laws (Mossuz-Lavau 1999, 331, 335). For many women activists, then, the 1975 abortion law was an important step, but it failed to go far enough. They protested the law's "protective" nature and thus continued to press for greater reproductive freedom. As we will see in chapter 4, one of their best weapons in this fight was the feminist press.

Despite its shortcomings, the 1975 abortion law was the outcome of a concerted effort by women's rights activists to fight the pervasive sexual inequalities that remained in all areas of women's social, political, and private lives. Already prior to 1975, increasing numbers of women had started to inquire into the causes of these inequalities. Many of them found a voice in Simone de Beauvoir, the renowned novelist and philosopher, who was the first to investigate the social conditions of French women. Her now classic assertion in *Le Deuxième sexe* that "one is not born, but rather becomes, woman" (2009, 293) shocked those who adhered to the traditional belief that "femininity" is a natural, biological destiny, not a cultural product. However, the purpose of Beauvoir's investigation was less to claim women's legal equality, admitted in principle, than to look at reality and help women recognize their status as the inferior, or second, sex. In this sense, her work contributed to consciousness-raising about women's oppression, an approach that later became the hallmark of the women's liberation movement. Beauvoir and her body of work became icons of the postwar feminist struggle for women's rights and exemplify how feminist high literature can participate in the creation of an empowered "sisterhood." In the following chapter, I will examine how Beauvoir engaged with the issue of body politics in French society.

2 Secondary Citizens

THIS CHAPTER EXAMINES how the French philosopher and novelist Simone de Beauvoir complicated and worked through projections of female corporeality in two of her major works, *Le Deuxième sexe* (1949) and *Les Belles images* (1966). My reading of these works presents Beauvoir as a feminist critic of French postwar consumer culture who forcefully wove together analysis of women's experiences with economic and social alienation and their objectification as wives and mothers. It is important to note that Beauvoir did not consider herself a "feminist" until after the publication of her major works in the 1970s, even though she had already become involved in the early stages of the women's liberation movement (Moi 1994, 211–12; Monteil 1997, 7–8). As we saw in the last chapter, she helped to write the famous "Manifesto of the 343" for the movement, publicly declaring that she was one of the 343 women who had undergone illegal abortions (Tristan and Pisan 1977, 63–69). Although the "manifesto" was a publicity stunt by the MLF, its publication in April 1971 contributed to making abortion a salient issue in Fifth Republic French politics.

By focusing on gender relations and corporeality in postwar France, my analysis of Beauvoir's work combines two new paths of inquiry that have recently sparked a veritable renaissance of Beauvoir studies on both sides of the Atlantic. The first, led by Margaret Simons, explores the philosophical relationship between Beauvoir and Jean-Paul Sartre, in whose shadow she undeservingly remained as a writer and public intellectual throughout her life (Simons 1995, 1999; Beauvoir 2004). The second examines the special role of the female body in Beauvoir's philosophy (Mackenzie 1986; Butler 1992; Arp 1995; Fishwick 1999–2000; Heinämaa 2003; Scarth 2004).

Building on these recent contributions, I analyze Beauvoir's description of the ways in which postwar consumer society constructed the female body as an object of consumer desire and show how this construction contributed to women's oppression and social and economic alienation. I will argue that her critical analysis of postwar consumer culture, which scholars have depicted as an example of politically engaged writing, advocates the feminist concept of "sisterhood" as a possible avenue for women to act collectively against sexual oppression (Kruks 2005; Marso 2006; Marso and Moynagh 2006; Shelby 2006). Here, Beauvoir's notion of "sisterhood" is grounded in the existentialist concept of "lived experience" (*l'expérience vécue*), the idea that women's identity is based not on fixed gender characteristics but rather on women's shared—albeit different—material experiences of pervasive gender constraints. Seen in this way, her contribution to the analysis of gender oppression became part of a historically specific feminist practice that used the construction of women's literal and metaphorical collectivity ("we") as a political tool to fight sexual oppression (Delphy 1984; Hawkesworth 1990; Milan Women's Bookstore Collective 1990; Zerilli 2005; Marso 2006, 152–53).

In order to better understand Beauvoir's unique contribution to feminist analysis, I will highlight in this chapter her claim that people construct human consciousness and agency along gendered corporeal lines—an understanding that challenged the disembodied concept of selfhood found in both the liberal concept of bourgeois individualism and Sartre's existentialism. To this end, I have divided the chapter into four sections. The first section briefly examines Beauvoir's aspirations as a writer. The second provides background information about the French postwar efforts at modernization, with a focus on the gendering of the developing consumer market but also discussing Beauvoir's theory of gender inequality, which draws heavily on descriptions of female corporeality in patriarchal culture. I will then turn to an analysis of the way in which Beauvoir portrayed and critiqued postwar gender roles in her novel *Les Belles images,* where she links ideas about the female body to bourgeois ideologies of consumerism, technology, advertisement, and fashion. I will investigate how Beauvoir's texts literally and metaphorically evoke and advocate the idea of "sisterhood," or female collectivity, as a political tool to build feminist consciousness and to effect social transformation through women's writing.

The idea of producing feminist identities through women's reading and writing has been explored by Virginia Sapiro (1992) and Wendy Gunther-Canada (2001) for another intellectual pioneer of feminism, Mary Wollstonecraft.[1] For the case of Beauvoir, Ann Curthoys (2000) has argued that contemporary women have used her novels and autobiographies as a veritable tool, or guide, for feminist self-fashioning (see also Marso 2006). In order to contextualize Beauvoir's feminist message, I shall begin with her experience as a female author in postwar France.

The Two Bodies of Simone de Beauvoir

Born in Paris in 1908 to a family of the haute bourgeoisie who eventually lost their financial resources, Simone de Beauvoir nevertheless enjoyed an elite education. Early in her life, she began to notice that society treated girls and boys differently and that marriage prospects for girls depended upon the size of the family fortune (Bair 1990). Toril Moi described Beauvoir as a "pioneering woman, . . . only the ninth woman in France to pass the *agrégation* examination in philosophy, and the youngest *agrégée* ever in that discipline, regardless of gender" (1994, 1). It was during the time of her studies at the university that Beauvoir met her lifelong partner, Jean-Paul Sartre, who just barely edged her out for first place in the final university examination and whose influence on French society as a writer and public intellectual would overshadow hers during their lifetime.

But Beauvoir's feminism made her a more controversial figure than Sartre. As Moi points out, "'Simone de Beauvoir' is not simply the name of a person who wrote novels, essays, and memoirs, but a site of ideological and aesthetic conflict" (1994, 74). In France and subsequently in the United States, readers put her into two distinct categories: a misguided female philosopher who had overstepped her intellectual boundaries, or a "feminist heroine" who advocated women's emancipation (Beauvoir 2009, xvii; see also Dijkstra 1980; Moi 1994, 73–84).

As Beauvoir became for (some of) her public a harmful moral and political influence, she exclaimed in an interview with Alice Jardine: "It's terrible, this tendency to consider women something dangerous to society" (Jardine 1979, 229). She also pointed out that men tended to use ambitious and successful women as an alibi to perpetuate the patriarchal order. She commented to Alice Schwarzer: "A woman in a position of power comes to resemble a man. She becomes a sort of token woman, and as such does men's work for them and even more effectively and more discreetly" (Schwarzer 1984, 97).

Throughout her career, however, Beauvoir often denied having suffered personally from unequal treatment or sexual discrimination as a woman. She stated in her autobiography: "I had never had any feeling of inferiority, no one had ever said to me: 'You think that way because you are a woman'; my femaleness had never been irksome to me in any way. 'For me,' I said to Sartre, 'you might almost say it just hasn't counted'" (Beauvoir 1992b, 94). Yet in the introduction to *The Second Sex*, written almost twenty years earlier, she wrote: "What is a woman? . . . Merely stating the problem suggests an immediate answer to me. It is significant that I pose it. It would never occur to a man to write a book on the singular situation of males in humanity. If I want to define myself, I first have to say, 'I am a woman'" (Beauvoir 2009, 5).

Beauvoir resolved this apparent contradiction in her thinking by making herself into an "exceptional" woman, one who had managed to escape the traps of bourgeois femininity—including motherhood—thanks to her special status as an intellectual (Schwarzer 1984, 36; Patterson 1986). Yet once she understood that the majority of women did not have this option, she turned her formidable talents to diagnosing the causes of this problem. In Beauvoir's understanding, the causes of women's secondary social status can be found in patriarchal culture, and in this specific instance, in the developing postwar mass consumer society, which upheld an inferior view of women's identity, or femininity. Before I turn to Beauvoir's feminist critique of postwar patriarchal culture, I will briefly provide important background information about the emerging French mass consumer society and its model of femininity.

Mass Consumerism and Gendered Corporeality in Postwar France

Although the French women's liberation movement grew out of the workers' and students' revolt of 1968, with their protests against the authoritarian structures of postwar society, autonomous women's groups had existed in Paris prior to the formation of the MLF. Instead of being one big group, "the" MLF consisted of a number of groups that differed greatly along ideological lines but were made up mostly of white, middle-class women much like Beauvoir herself (Duchen 1986; Allwood and Wadia 2000). Why did these "privileged" women feel that they needed help? In comparative terms, France had a high percentage of women in the labor force during the late 1940s and early 1950s, on whom the burgeoning consumer society imposed a double burden of employment and household duties. Women in postwar France had been turned into exploited, unpaid workers. New household technologies permeated the domestic sphere, domestic servants had largely vanished, and specialized commercial agencies had started to disappear. As

Ruth Schwartz Cowan (1983) notes in her study of the "industrial revolution" in the home, the number of household tasks increased as the number of household servants declined. Ironically, the technologies that were supposed to simplify domestic work actually created more of it. Cowan writes: "We do have various time studies, which demonstrate somewhat surprisingly that housewives with conveniences were spending just as much time on household duties as were housewives without them; housework, like so many other types of work, expands to fill the available time" (40–41).

The explosion of the mass consumer society in the 1940s and 1950s, which included the producers of goods, the advertising agents who promoted them, and the periodicals that published the promotions, spread an ideology of consumer practice that contributed to the objectification of women in the home. Advertisers showed women with consumer items such as radios and washing machines, using sex appeal to sell products and thereby turning women themselves into consumer items. The women in these ads were in charge of household purchases, such as kitchen equipment and dining ware, which again made them appear to be mere objects of the home, rather than individuals with needs and rights. In a striking parallel, when President Charles de Gaulle finally decreed French women's right to vote in 1944, he presented this right as "continuing a feminine tradition of duty and thinking of others" rather than acknowledging women's inalienable rights as citizens (Duchen 1994, 35). He thereby reinforced the idea that motherhood and the care of children and the home defined womanhood.

Despite the increase in individual consumption, most of the population failed to experience a general change in social status or social mobility. According to Susan E. Weiner, "the gap between media images of the home and its appliances and actual living conditions was never fully closed for most people" (1995, 125). As some critics argued, French postwar modernization was part reality, part fiction (Ross 1995; Stanley 2008).

One major site in the "fiction of consumerism" was the newly emerging genre of women's magazines. These publications informed women about their proper role as consumers and in turn codified the postwar image of the woman as homemaker even though women were increasingly participating in the labor market. Because of their overlapping roles at home and at work, women became ideal targets for the expanding consumer markets promoted in these magazines. Women's periodicals such as *Marie Claire* (1937) and *Elle* (1945) sought to combine images of both the woman at home and the working mother to create a slightly revamped feminine ideal (Duchen 1994, 117). As we will see in chapter 3, these magazines specifically promoted bodily self-fashioning as part of a new feminist project depicting the beautiful (i.e., fit and slender) body as a "liberated" body. Thus, these women's periodicals supported claims to a universal femininity even as they appropriated liberal feminism for their own self-definition and promotional ends.

A few examples will demonstrate this point. For instance, *Elle* regularly featured reports on the women's liberation movement and the role of women in politics (Rudder 1980; Carretier 1983), yet the magazine often contradicted its emancipatory message for women because, like all for-profit mass magazines, it had to conflate politics and consumerism in order to sell (Sullerot 1963; Dardigna 1979; Ferguson 1983; Bonvoisin and Maignien 1986; Winship 1987; Ballaster 1991; McCracken 1993; Scanlon 1995). An issue from March 1986, while examining the exploitation of women who operated telephone sex lines, called *standardistes perverses,* featured an ad depicting the gigantic mouth of a woman lusting for a bowl of pasta. Next to the bowl was a telephone number with a suggestive caption: "Call me and I will tell you about the many delicious ways in which you can use this new pasta from Rivoire & Carret" (Corre 1986; Rivoire and Carret 1986). It is difficult to determine what the editors hoped to accomplish by mixing texts, images, and advertisements in this way, which equates a critique of traditional, patriarchal values with consumer ideology. As we shall see, the conflation of politics and consumption in popular magazines, including women's magazines, illustrates the expansion of the marketplace into the realm of the political, where readers are accorded the status of free (and equal) consumers, however limited this freedom might be (Featherstone 1991; Berlant 1997). (As we also shall see, the appropriation of the term "choice" for a woman's right to an abortion echoes this development in the area of reproductive politics.)

The domestic life of the "new woman" depicted in these magazines did not differ much from the lives of women in earlier years. But these periodicals, together with other aspects of the media, now inundated women with expert advice and advertisements about household organization, cooking, parenting, marriage, fashion, and hygiene: "Housewives were turned into amateurs, no longer able to trust their own way of doing things or follow the advice handed down from grandmother and mother. The expert was brought in to show women what to do" (Duchen 1994, 71).[2] Husbands seemed essentially uninvolved in concerns about the house and children, leaving the impression that the responsibility for the modern family rested squarely on the shoulders of the wives and mothers (ibid., 87, 99).

Not surprisingly, cutting-edge intellectuals, from Roland Barthes to Guy Debord, Jean Baudrillard, and Simone de Beauvoir, targeted these new cultural assumptions. Beauvoir was possibly the first theorist to analyze gender relations and the discourse on motherhood in French postwar society. In *The Second Sex,* where she penned the now classic dictum "One is not born, but rather becomes, woman" (2009, 293), she pioneered the now relatively common belief that femininity is socially constructed. Demonstrating that male-dominated society imposes gender roles upon both women and men, she showed how these gender roles are constructed in part through social institutions of the private sphere, such as marriage, motherhood, and the family, which subjugate women through oppressive conventions of femininity created and reproduced throughout history. She thus argued that women's liberation must begin with the transformation of the social institutions that perpetuate social conventions, keep women separate from one another, and mask women's common struggle (Marso 2006, 150, 152).

Writing about the institution of marriage, for instance, Beauvoir showed that she was aware of the dominant role it played in the life of most women: "The destiny that society traditionally offers women is marriage. Even today, most women are, were, or plan to be married, or they suffer from not being so. Marriage is the reference by which the single woman is defined, whether she is frustrated, disgusted, or even indifferent to this institution" (2009, 451). Married women were of necessity preoccupied with housework and child-rearing tasks, which, she felt, could never provide a sense of real fulfillment because they merely kept a woman busy and perpetuated the idea that she was the servant of others (Schwarzer 1984, 42). She also argued that gender inequality was built on biological difference, forcing women and men to experience their bodies differently:

> [A woman's body] is a burden: weakened by the species, bleeding every month, passively propagating, for her it is not the pure instrument of her grasp on the world but rather an opaque presence; it is not certain that it will give her pleasure and it creates pains that tear her apart; it contains threats: she feels danger in her "insides." Her body is "hysterical" because of the close connection between endocrine secretions and nervous and sympathetic systems commanding muscles and viscera; it expresses reactions the woman refuses to accept: in sobs, convulsions, and vomiting, her body escapes her, it betrays her; it is her most intimate reality, but it is a shameful reality that she keeps hidden. And yet it is her marvellous double; she contemplates it in the mirror with amazement; it is the promise of happiness, a work of art, a living statue; she shapes it, adorns it, displays it. (2009, 672)

Feminist and antifeminist thinkers alike have criticized Beauvoir's representation of the female body as repugnant and handicapped (Moi 1994, chap. 6). By contrast, Sarah Fishwick (1999–2000, 55) claims that Beauvoir treated the female body in inherently ambiguous terms, oscillating between reductive biological stereotyping and critical elaboration of controlling cultural practices in order to prove her theoretical point about gender relations. When discussing the gendered female body in *The Second Sex,* Beauvoir argued that patriarchal society predefines the way in which women experience their bodies. In this way, women's bodies become the raw material that men interpret and "gender"—as in, for instance, the cultural icons of the maternal and virginal body. As a result, rather than shaping or fashioning their own bodies, women view them as a material reality beyond the possibility of change or choice. Beauvoir has called women's experience of their "always already" gendered identity "lived experience," foregrounding the socially dominant imagery of female corporeality as limited, and even repulsive (Holveck 2002).

At the same time that Beauvoir demonstrated that women's bodies are a locus for patriarchal power, she also suggested the possible avenues for women to resist this power. If, as she contested, women's bodies (and thereby gender) are culturally produced and contingent, rather than a biological given, then women need to assume two things to reverse gender inequalities: first, subjectivity or selfhood; and second, political agency. In a later interview, she echoed this call for female agency:

> Women in greater numbers [should] refuse to allow themselves to be considered any longer as natural property to be controlled or dominated. Women will turn to feminism for their self-education, and the fight will begin. It will be a hard struggle because men will not easily surrender their freedom from housework and family responsibility and all the other burdens that typify women's lot today. . . . I think that when women really begin to consider liberating themselves seriously, they will take more of an interest in politics. And since liberation is a democratic concept, they will become more democratic and thus more radical. Men must be made to understand that, in the final analysis, feminist behavior is not gratuitous but serious. Feminists are not useless and silly hysterics. They have studied and thought, and they want to make changes that will benefit all of society. (Bair 1986, 162)

In the following section, we will see how Beauvoir uncovers the nexus between female corporeality and consumer culture for her advocacy of female agency in her novel *Les Belles images,* set in 1960s France. Here, following Fishwick, I interpret Beauvoir's idea about the abject female body less as a biologically reductive concept than as the result of how she observed the ways that women experience pervasive gender constraints in material terms.

Beauvoir's Feminist Critique of Female Corporeality in Les Belles Images

Beauvoir's theory of gendered embodiment surfaces strongly in her last novel, *Les Belles images,* published in 1966. The book's success in France was based partly on the author's ability to satirize the new "techno-bourgeoisie," made up of engineers, bureaucrats (*cadres*), and media and advertisement producers. The story revolves around Laurence, a married advertisement executive and mother of two daughters, who lives in Paris and allegedly embodies the new "liberated" workingwoman. But her sheltered, petit bourgeois life is disturbed when one of her daughters, Catherine, begins to experience anxiety attacks.

Looking for solutions to her daughter's apparent distress, Laurence is disappointed both by her husband's suggestion that she simply consult a child psychologist and by her father's outright reluctance to help. In contrast to the two men, she feels deeply implicated in Catherine's emotional crisis, partially because she fears being blamed for her daughter's "illness" by her family and friends. Laurence's fear of being seen as the cause of Catherine's emotional troubles can be explained by the ways in which parental obligations are constructed socially along gendered lines. In the modern nuclear family, mothers assume responsibility for the physical and emotional well-being of the rest of the family, especially the children, who are commonly expected to surpass their parents' accomplishments. Laurence's fear of being blamed for her child's emotional issues thus represents her broader anxieties about being judged a failure as a mother (and wife), which, as Beauvoir explained so poignantly in her theoretical work about the social construction of gender, is represented to women as their sole acceptable role or destiny.

Laurence soon slips into her own crisis of depression, which is aggravated by an eating disorder that inscribes her fears onto her body. In the process of resolving her identity crisis, she ultimately becomes disillusioned with the two men in her life, who represent continuity and change in modern France: her father, who embodies the old bourgeoisie, and her husband, a member of the new techno-bourgeoisie. At the end of the novel, Laurence is ready to take charge of her daughters' lives, but her resolve ultimately remains ambiguous: "No, she cried aloud. Not Catherine. I shan't let what has been done to me be done to her. What have they made of me? . . . As far as I am concerned, the game's over, she thought, looking at her reflection—rather white and haggard. But the children will have their chance. What chance? She did not even know" (Beauvoir 1968, 222, 224).

In this novel, Beauvoir portrays the female protagonist, Laurence, as a smart consumer of images and objects through her work as an advertising executive, and also as a regular reader of women's magazines. She seems keenly aware of mass consumerism, as the opening scene of the book, depicting a family visit to the countryside, makes abundantly clear: "At this very moment in another garden, wholly different and exactly the same, someone else is saying these words and the same smile is forming on another face: 'What a wonderful Sunday!' Why do I think that?" (Beauvoir 1968, 10). At the same time, Laurence is afraid that she lacks individuality, that she is simply like everybody else in her social class. While having dinner with friends and family, she looks around and asks herself: "What have the others got that I haven't?" (9). Her tendency to echo the attitudes of a typical bourgeois lifestyle becomes clear in another countryside scene, where her mother, Dominique, inquires how her guests are enjoying the visit: "'A happy day, my pets?' asked Dominique. 'Wonderful,' cried Marthe earnestly. 'Wonderful,' repeated Laurence" (18). And again: "'A thoroughly successful weekend!' said Jean-Charles. 'Thoroughly successful' [replied Laurence]" (23).[3]

By describing Laurence as a consumer of images and objects, Beauvoir sets up two major polarities in the story. While women are traditionally associated with nature, the role they play in her representation of postwar France is emblematic of an unnatural, artificial consumer culture. Her representation must be read against the backdrop of postwar French social relations, which she so successfully satirizes in the novel. As Susan E. Weiner (1995, 130, 131, 142) has observed, by the mid-1950s, French women's new identity as consumers had seemingly inverted the image of the passive female. Women were now constructed as active, if not aggressive, shoppers who ventured outside the private sphere. And, curiously, all of the female characters in Beauvoir's novel suffer in one way or another from "overconsumption."[4] Laurence's mother, for instance, experiences loneliness and a lack of love after leaving Laurence's father for a rich businessman. In Laurence's case, her eating disorder is less a form of revolt against the standards of society than her realization that she completely identifies with the "belles images," or pretty pictures, of that culture represented on television and in fashion and news magazines (Penrod 1987).

Consequently, Laurence feels trapped in a body that repulses her, a situation that triggers repeated bouts of nausea. This "nausea" represents the fact that she cannot resist being manipulated by others. This term is crucial. Jean-Paul Sartre had used this key idea in his novel of the same name, *La Nausée* (1938). Like Sartre's main character, Roquentin, the protagonist in *Les Belles images,* Laurence, suffers from spells of nausea, which symbolize her developing awareness of the emptiness and meaninglessness of a life made up solely of objects or matter. For both Sartre and Beauvoir, individual consciousness is ceaselessly trying to escape this emptiness to construct subjective meaning.

However, Beauvoir's notion of "nausea" differs from Sartre's in an important way. For Sartre, nausea was a sentiment that heralded the first steps toward existential revolt, whereas Beauvoir treats this experience as a graphically *material* sensation that wracks the totality of the body: "a spasm wrenched her stomach and she vomited all the tea she had just drunk. It had not happened to her for years, being sick from emotion" (1968, 149). Toward the end of the novel, Laurence's feelings of entrapment are expressed in the following way: "They would force her to eat; they would force her to swallow it all. All what? All that she vomited out, her life, the lives of the others with their phony loves, their stories about money, their lies. . . . What have they made of me? This woman who loves no one, who is indifferent to the beauties of the world, who cannot even weep—this woman that I vomit forth" (221, 222). As Laurence becomes increasingly aware that she is feeding off "the glossy veneer of the world in which she lives" (Holland 1998–99, 121), symbolized by the central importance of food and eating in the novel, she decides to do something about it and help her daughters avoid a similar fate (Fallaize 1988; Patterson 1989; Holland 1998–99; Corbí Saéz 2008–2009).

As María Isabel Corbí Saéz informs us in her linguistic study of *Les Belles images* (2008–2009, 21), Laurence's resolve to empower herself and to take an affirmative stance on behalf of her daughters' life is symbolized in the novel through her "capture of speech" (*prise de parole*)—her refusal to reproduce the male dominant discourse on feminine ideals and expectations and her insistence instead on expressing her own point of view. Corbí Saéz suggests that Laurence's attempt to step into individual subjectivity (or what Beauvoir refers to in *The Second Sex* as no longer living in "bad faith" [2009, 773]) through the "capture of speech" foreshadows the protest tactics of the women's liberation movement, which used the written and spoken word in its demands for women's equal citizenship rights.[5] I should like to go farther and say that Laurence's symbolic struggle for self-expression, for individual consciousness and agency, is embodied in her distinctly *physical* experience of nausea and convulsions. This bodily experience suggests that for women in our society, gender identity is grounded in the body, and female corporeality must be taken into consideration if anything is to change politically—if women are to gain any meaningful political agency in postwar consumer culture.[6] In *Les Belles images,* Beauvoir seems to suggest a way for women to recognize their shared experiences of oppression, or common bond of "sisterhood," as a possible basis for collective action. In the book, this is exemplified in Laurence's decision to support her daughter's friendship with her best school friend (Corbí Saéz 2008–2009, 26–27).

From Living in "Bad Faith" to Constructing Women's "Sisterhood"

For Beauvoir, "bad faith" was a reference to women's complicity in their own subjugation to male domination when they accept being relegated to secondary status. In her opinion, in order to become liberated, it was necessary for women to "refus[e] to be the Other," which would involve renouncing "all the advantages an alliance with the superior caste confers on them" (2009, 10). Analyzing male privilege, she declared: "She [woman] determines and differentiates herself in relation to man, and he does in relation to her; she is the inessential in front of the essential. He is the Subject, he is the Absolute. She is the Other" (6).

As we have seen, according to Beauvoir, a woman's role as a man's Other is experienced through her estrangement from her body: "[Woman] feels . . . that her body is an alienated opaque thing; it is the prey of a stubborn and foreign life that makes and unmakes a crib in her every month; every month a child is prepared to be born and is aborted in the flow of the crimson tide; woman *is* her body as man *is* his but her body is something other than her" (2009, 42; emphasis in original). It was for this reason that Beauvoir felt that a woman's freedom was dependent upon her ability to control her own body. In specific terms, she believed that unwanted pregnancies interfered with a woman's ability to be independent, economically as well as otherwise. (In order to gain economic independence, Beauvoir advocated that women leave the confines of the home to obtain employment.) As she stated in *The Second Sex:*

> Men universally forbid abortion; but they accept it individually as a convenient solution; they can contradict themselves with dizzying cynicism; but woman feels the contradictions in her wounded flesh; she is generally too shy to deliberately revolt against masculine bad faith; while seeing herself as a victim of an injustice that decrees her to be a criminal in spite of herself, she still feels dirtied and humiliated. . . . Stekel said it correctly: 'Prohibition of abortion is an immoral law, since it must be forcibly broken every day, every hour.' Birth control and legal abortion would allow women to control their pregnancies freely. (2009, 545–46)

In her insistence on the primacy of the body for individual rights, Beauvoir differed greatly from other liberal feminist critics before her, such as Britain's Mary Wollstonecraft and American temperance feminists Susan B. Anthony and Elizabeth Cady Stanton, who had also denounced the ill effects of consumerism on women's existence. According to historian Karen Offen (1988, 142), Beauvoir's liberal theories offered contemporary feminists a new line of argument: in contrast to earlier feminist strategies evoking motherhood as an ideal role and identity for women in an attempt to get the government to enact laws protecting women and children, her contemporaries fought to end governmental control over women's fertility and their bodies by challenging existing laws dealing with issues such as abortion.

Seen in this way, Beauvoir's theoretical works held great potential for women's collective political agency in Fifth Republic France. Although her texts have been criticized for devaluing feminine activities such as bearing and rearing children, they explore women's social situation and have helped women become more aware of their situation in male-dominated society. Despite the fact that Beauvoir presented her ideas in abstract existentialist concepts, for many women in postwar France she was able to capture and articulate the essence of their continued oppression (Dijkstra 1980). She employed the philosophical concept of "lived experience" to explain women's situation as at the same time free ("transcendent") and constrained ("immanent") by historically specific social and economic forces. Her usage of this concept shows how she applied her broader philosophical framework to explain the specific situation of women's oppression, that is, how social institutions, discourses, and practices enable yet limit women's individual agency (Vintges 1995). In particular, her philosophical framework reflects her radical political view that far-reaching social reforms were necessary to bring about women's liberation. It is for this reason that she argued that women lack the means to organize collectively to change their lot and to change society primarily because they live "dispersed among men, tied by homes, work, economic interests, and social conditions to certain men—fathers or husbands—more closely than to other women" (2009, 8).

This is certainly the case for Laurence, the female protagonist in *Les Belles images,* who, until she actively resolves to change her daughters' situation, is first portrayed by Beauvoir as living in "bad faith" because she denies her own freedom, blames others for her unhappiness, and even lies about it to herself. Although she has attachments to a number of female family members and friends, including her mother, Dominique, her sister, Marthe, and a friend at work, Mona, she is most influenced by the men in her life, particularly her father.

When Laurence encounters problems in her life, she first seeks the advice of her husband, Jean-Charles, and her father, whom she trusts to make sound judgments based on his "authentic" moral values, and is much less interested in the views and experiences of the women around her. Her mother, for instance, is portrayed as so dependent on the men in her life that she would rather commit suicide than live alone. And in Laurence's eyes, her sister has long since lost touch with reality as a result of her deep religious convictions. Likewise, she sees her friend Mona as incapable of understanding her feelings of alienation because Mona is generally uncritical of her surroundings. Women are thus forced to behave according to certain gender ideals, which keep them from developing a shared understanding of, or solidarity with, their situation. By living in "bad faith," women themselves perpetuate the male standards and expectations that oppress them. This is the case with Laurence, who dismisses her mother's and sister's life choices as "failures."

If women would only recognize their shared, yet not identical, experiences, Beauvoir suggests, they could begin to explore the power of a political "sisterhood" that charts alternative ways to organize society and social institutions. In a 1984 interview many years after the publication of *Les Belles images,* she talked about these politics of "sisterhood":

> In mass action, women can have power. The more women become conscious of the need for mass action, the more progress will be achieved. And, as to the woman who can afford to seek individual liberation, the more she can influence her friends and sisters, and the more that consciousness will spread, which in turn, when frustrated by the system, will stimulate mass action. Of course, the more that consciousness spreads, the more men will be aggressive and violent. But then, the more men are aggressive, the more will women need other women to fight back. That is, the need for mass action will be clear. (Bair 1986, 160)

It is through such vital insights that Beauvoir's work offered new categories of analysis to women to contest their secondary status and to become political agents (Brosman 1991, 37, 38; Ward 1995; Tidd 1999, 45, 46, 57; Curthoys 2000; Kruks 2005).

While Beauvoir believed that women could liberate themselves through collective action, on the surface it seems that *Les Belles images* lacks any consciousness of a female "sisterhood." But in many ways, the novel makes a strong case for a shared feminine identity: Beauvoir suggests that women are particularly vulnerable to the power of the image because they have traditionally been its objects rather than its creators. In this way, women's political agency is intrinsically connected to the standards of male society, which potentially oppresses all women.

Laurence's verbal confrontation with her husband at the end of the novel represents an example of a woman who is fighting gender conventions and who is finding the words to represent her own point of view: "In spite of herself Laurence's voice was rising; she talked on and on, she was not quite sure what she was saying but it did not matter—what did matter was to shout louder than Jean-Charles and all the others and to reduce them to silence. Her heart was beating furiously, her eyes blazed. 'I have made my decisions, and I shall not yield.' . . . If I stand firm I shall win. 'If you want war, war it shall be'" (Beauvoir 1968, 223, 224). Here Laurence realizes that her husband and father have let her down, and she resolves to take matters into her own hands with a veritable "call to arms" (reminiscent of Madame de Merteuil's challenge to Valmont in *Les Liaisons dangereuses*) to save her daughters from the clutches of an unjust society.[7] The reader may well recognize not only her own feelings of powerlessness but also the fact that Laurence's task will be too challenging for her to carry out alone. Beauvoir's protagonist is thus likely to find potential "sisters-in-arms" in the readers of the book.

The success of Beauvoir's work touches upon an important question in the history of feminism: Do books such as *The Second Sex* and *Les Belles images* influence the way that women think and act? In Fifth Republic France, the emerging women's liberation movement appropriated not only Beauvoir's theoretical insights about women's oppression, but also her view that writing can contribute to raising the political awareness of the oppressed. While Beauvoir (1992a, 111, 271) acknowledged in her memoirs, for instance, that she would use her written work to speak on behalf of the oppressed, she nevertheless considered herself "apolitical," meaning that she would not join a political movement. Similarly, she downplayed her role in influencing the development of the women's liberation movement in France. In an interview in 1976, she stated:

> The current feminist movement, which really started five or six years ago, did not really know [*The Second Sex*]. Then, as the movement grew, some of the leaders took from it some of their theoretical basis. But *The Second Sex* in no way launched the feminist movement. Most of the women who became very active in the movement were much too young in 1949–50, when the book came out, to be influenced by it. What pleases me, of course, is that they discovered it later. . . . They may have become feminists for the reasons I explain in *The Second Sex*; but they discovered the reasons in their life experiences, not in my book. (Gerassi 1976, 79)

Beauvoir's statement that women come to feminism not because of a particular book but rather because of the "lived experience" they share in a patriarchal society, I believe, expresses both her humility as a writer and her acknowledgment of the importance of existentialist philosophy to her theory of gender oppression. Beauvoir had explained that women lacked the opportunities and means through which they could develop a sense of self and personal autonomy necessary for individual agency. If, for her, writing functioned as a vehicle to engender individual subjectivity (as she acknowledged in her memoirs that it had), then writing could possibly function as an avenue to raise women's feminist consciousness and—perhaps—lead to collective political action based on it (Beauvoir 1992a, 271). It is in this sense that I understand her willingness in 1971 to help craft the political "manifesto" for the MLF, which increased public awareness about illegal abortions in France and propelled demands for women's rights onto the political agenda—an outcome that she could not have foreseen but that she obviously welcomed as a politically engaged writer.

To conclude: What set Beauvoir's political thought apart and made her an icon of French postwar feminist activism and scholarship was her insight that the female body serves as an important locus of patriarchal power in Western culture and the implication of this insight into the constitutive "nature" of the body as always already gendered. Importantly, her pioneering analysis of the nexus of consumer culture and women's bodily agency, particularly the pathologies of dominant body images, offered far-reaching opportunities for women, as they could see the importance of acting collectively to resist patriarchal power relations through the very gendered embodiment that defines women.

At the same time, however, as Beauvoir and the MLF promoted the political empowerment of women through the act of writing, and as they mounted a critique of postwar consumer society and its debilitating concept of femininity, the market for women's fashion magazines exploded in postwar France, giving women unexpected access to information on how to cultivate femininity through the consumption of beauty and fashion products. Without a doubt, these magazines also believed in the power of writing for women, as they sought to create their own sense of "sisterhood" among their readership. The representation of commercialized womanhood (and especially its focus on the female body) in such mass cultural texts, as well as the appropriation of feminist ideas of self-fashioning and choice for their own promotional ends, will be the subject of the following chapter.

3 Citizen Consumers

IN NOVEMBER 1970, the women's magazine *Elle* staged a unique publicity event outside Paris. The magazine's staff organized a series of conferences or meetings, called a "Women's General Assembly" (États généraux de la femme), with the objective to zero in on French women's expectations for social change, and to bring their claims to the attention of the political elite. The assembly's meetings were preceded by the distribution of some 8,000 surveys to *Elle* readers throughout France. Now the time had come to take stock and to discuss what, according to these surveys, French women had identified as their foremost concerns in "all areas of the female condition" (Pringle 1995, 145). *Elle* planned to collect and make available the conclusions reached by the attending women and invited "experts" (including politicians, academics, and social activists) in the form of a "white book" to further women's sociopolitical rights. With this self-proclaimed aspiration for women's emancipation, *Elle* wanted to give its readers (who presumably represented all French women) a voice to challenge the sexual and political inequalities between women and men that persisted in postwar France (Wadia 1991; Pringle 1995; Colombani and Fitoussi 2005).

In this chapter, I explore how popular magazines for women (and men) functioned in post-1945 France as ideological sites for producing and reproducing social gender ideals and identities. Specifically, I argue that popular magazines such as the French *Elle* can help mediate changing societal attitudes about women's gender roles as well as women's experiences as political agents who vindicate and enact these changes, as exemplified by *Elle*'s organization of the "Women's General Assembly" in 1970. In the case of *Elle*, the magazine promoted the law on contraception as early as 1961, the laws on abortion in 1975 (the Veil law) and 1979 (the Pelletier law), the legalization of the morning-after pill in the 1980s, and political activism to redress the rise of the antiabortion movement in France in the late 1980s to 1990s (Wadia 1991, 273; Elle 1995; Colombani and Fitoussi 2005).

In France, popular women's magazines, which started to mushroom after World War II, soon became an avenue for women to engage in political activism and agency by offering them a social space in which to exchange opinions and personal experiences on a wide range of topics, including matters of sexuality and reproduction. In the pages of these magazines, women could find and read information about reproductive rights, and they could discuss their personal circumstances and experiences with reproduction through written contributions to the magazines' letter page or readers' forum, for instance. Following Pnina Werbner (1999, 223), I call such a discursive space an "imagined sisterhood," a space that expresses a shared female identity and a sense of community among women.[1] In this way, women's magazines, like other types of women's writings, helped develop the French postwar women's liberation movement in the 1970s and 1980s. In the case of *Elle,* the magazine expressed its solidarity with the MLF and thereby contributed to the postwar women's rights debate. In turn, the MLF affected French postwar gender politics in a unique way because it made reproductive freedom the central focus in its struggle for women's equal citizenship rights.

One important way in which women's magazines contributed to women's political activism is by creating political meaning through the act of reading. Instead of being the cultural dupes of media institutions, readers of popular magazines could seek and find not just entertainment but also guidance, including guidance on coping with patriarchal culture. Theorists such as Stuart Hall and Michel de Certeau have demonstrated the subversive nature of popular magazines and of popular culture in general (Hall and Jefferson 1976; Certeau 1984; Jenkins 1992). Ruth Rosen (2000, 313), however, has pointed to some of the limitations of popular women's empowerment, calling the type of feminine agency cultivated in women's magazines "consumer feminism" because it looks for individual rather than collective responses to women's problems and because it usually ignores larger economic and social obstacles that women can face. I agree with Rosen and Berlant, who have shown how publications such as *Elle* conflate politics and consumerism by advancing a type of women's empowerment that rests squarely on consumption. In this way, women's magazines can be seen as constructing ambivalent notions of femininity, which are then imparted to readers as "natural" rather than created (Redstocking Sister 1971; Berlant 1997; Rosen 2000). In describing the type of feminine agency promoted by *Elle,* one commentator offered the following description: "Decked out from head to toe, the purse strapped around the shoulder, they [women] dress up to conquer their independence" (Pringle 1995, 14).

In historical terms, as Lisa Tiersten (2001) has pointed out, the "woman consumer" became controversial and contested as soon as she appeared in late nineteenth-century France, as she embodied the complex relations between the republic and the expanding market, expressing concerns that commerce and industry threatened republican ideals. The figure of the female consumer, *la consommatrice,* is best captured by the French writers Gustave Flaubert ([1896] 1995) and Elsa Triolet (1959) in their respective novels *Madame Bovary* and *Roses à crédit,* in which the female protagonists' acts of overconsumption embody the collapse of the distinction between the private and political spheres through market relationships. Women's magazines helped create this figure by giving women advice on how and what to consume. But they also provided advice on how to deal with male-dominated society, thereby offering women a shared sense of community: in effect, these magazines assumed that all women shared these political concerns—and wanted to consume as well.

In contemporary women's magazines, a good example of this practice emerges in the fictional community of the letter page (as well as in the inclusive use of the "editorial we"). In these heavily mediated discussions, women readers create a common bond through an exchange of experiences with and opinions on a variety of issues. As Janice Winship, who has studied the ideological function of women's magazines, remarks: "The readers' letters and editorial responses often reveal a profound commitment to the 'individual solution' [as opposed to collective action]. Both teach the same parable: individual effort will overcome all odds" (1987, 76).

A letter written by "Isabelle" to the French *Elle,* dated March 9, 1987, demonstrates this point. "Isabelle" writes: "I am single and happy with my life, I earn a good living, I am not ugly, I know how to dress well, I have a job I like, in a nutshell, I love my life. My problem: the men I get to know are turned off by me. They invite me to dinner, they court me, they comport themselves as perfect gentlemen, yet suddenly they tell me that I frighten them! They ask me out less and less and then disappear completely without even asking to have sex with me! It's incomprehensible. I always make clear that I am neither looking to get married nor to have children. What is it that frightens them?" (Ségal 1987). In their response, the editors lecture Isabelle about men's nature ("they don't want to be told off before they even begin the chase") and give her more practical advice about keeping her ideas about marriage and motherhood a secret until she has "caught" one of the men (ibid.). Thus Isabelle's problem (and, by extension, those of other readers as well) is "solved" without questioning broader attitudes about women and men's roles in society.

Ironically, women's magazines' construction of an "imagined" sisterhood of readers at times created "real" political spaces, such as the "Women's General Assembly," instituted by the magazine *Elle* in 1970 with the intention to make the (male) political elite pay attention to women's needs. To tease out how women's magazines, and in this case the market leader, *Elle,* participated in constructing feminine subjects and spaces in postwar France, I have divided this chapter into two sections. The first section furnishes important theoretical material for understanding how female and male identities are socially produced and reproduced through mass print media. It also provides a brief history of French women's magazines in order to contextualize their role and importance in shaping postwar French gender and sexual politics. The second section analyzes how one sample magazine, *Elle,* situated itself as a major political player in the postwar debate about reproductive rights and how it engaged its readers as potential political actors in this debate.

Before we proceed, a few methodological remarks about content analysis are in order. This chapter focuses on one major French women's magazine, *Elle,* which, together with *Marie Claire, Marie France,* and *Femmes d'aujourd'hui,* targeted female consumers in the flourishing fashion and beauty magazine market after World War II. Founded in 1945, *Elle* quickly became a market leader, and by 1965 it was read by one in eight French women (Pringle 1995, 15). Over the years, its weekly circulation numbers fluctuated between 300,000 and 600,000, but seem steady today at about 350,000 copies (exceeded only by *Marie Claire* and the French edition of *Cosmopolitan*).[2] However, *Elle* was chosen for this study not just because of its prominence in the competitive women's magazine market, but also because of its self-proclaimed emancipatory agenda "to assist women in conquering their independence" (Pringle 1995, 14). (Today, *Elle*'s ongoing mission to emancipate women through information is evident in the magazine's charitable enterprise, the ELLE Foundation [La Fondation d'entreprise ELLE], which was created in 2004.)[3] In comparison to its competitors at the time, *Elle* was the more modern fashion and beauty magazine and therefore was more open to new ideas, including feminist ideas. In addition, from its inception, it was aimed at young, oftentimes working, middle-class women who were receptive to feminist ideas. By the early 1970s, more than 50 percent of *Elle*'s readers were between the ages of 15 and 35, and more than 60 percent were employed (Wadia 1991, 263).

My content analysis of *Elle* covers the years from 1970 to 1992, which are considered the height of French second-wave feminism. In those twenty-three years, *Elle* published roughly 2,000 issues. For each issue I examined the text and illustrations of the magazine's "general features" (articles, reports, editorials) as well as the copy and illustrations of paid advertisements. No formal coding was undertaken; instead, my examination focused on references to feminist ideas of the women's liberation movement that readers would encounter while skimming or "moving around" in the magazine's general features and advertisements—a typical reading process for popular media such as women's magazines (Hazan 1986, 214). The feminist ideas referenced can be encapsulated in two main categories: advice on women's reproductive rights (contraception and abortion) and women's political activism (agency). Paid advertisements were included in the study because purchased advertising space can make up as much as 50 to 60 percent of a women's magazine's issue, and because advertisers have a strong hand in demanding "supportive" copy and editorials to promote readers' consumption (Lipovetsky 1977, 159; Cantor 1987; Farrell 1994, 622).

Overall, my study of *Elle* from 1970 to 1992 shows that the feminist movement provided the magazine with a unique opportunity to address women's need for political advice and agency. Specifically, references to feminist ideas of the women's liberation movement (and reports about the MLF, of course) allowed the magazine to contribute to the postwar debate about women's citizenship rights, which the movement summed up in its demand for a woman's right to control her own body. However, a closer look at the narratives employed in editorial features and paid advertisements reveals that *Elle* participated in the construction of ideas about feminine agency that were ambivalent at times, as the magazine conflated two seemingly contradictory social arenas: consumerism and politics. The following section furnishes important background information on the role of popular magazines, including women's magazines, in the creation of such a consumer culture in postwar France.

Inside Women's Magazines

It is necessary to view postwar women's magazines within a broader historical context, for this helps to illustrate both the continuities and the striking changes within the genre after World War II. Women's magazines were first introduced to French readers with the short-lived *Courrier de la nouveauté:*

Feuille hebdomadaire à l'usage des dames (from 1758) and *Le Journal des dames* (1797–1839). At the time, these early publications filled an important need, offering advice to women on how to be feminine. But because they represented the aristocratic notion of femininity, they were limited in their scope and reported mainly on court gossip; the point was to provide reading material for ladies of the leisured classes. Later on, during the French Revolution, women's traditional roles were less neatly defined, and that fact led to publications that dealt largely with the issue of educating girls and women. By contrast, under the Restoration (1814–30), women's periodicals multiplied by bridging the two previous trends: women's magazines with a focus on fashion advice, on the one hand, and those with a focus on the education of girls and women, on the other. More often than not, these magazines used the term "fashion" (*mode*) in their titles, which quickly distinguished them from "feminist" publications. The latter flourished after the Revolution of 1830 and under the influence of Saint-Simonian socialism (Adler 1979). Following Louis-Napoléon's coup d'état of 1851, feminist journals died out (and were not revived until thirty years later) and women's emancipation receded into thin air. However, during the period of the Second Empire (1852–70), fashion magazines such as *Le Conseiller des dames* and *La Mode illustrée* kept upper-class women busy with advice on housekeeping, etiquette, and handicraft projects that sometimes took them weeks to complete (Sullerot 1963).

Following the return of democratic institutions under the Third Republic (1870–1940), French society experienced a veritable boom in women's magazines. It was during this period, often called the *belle époque* of the women's press, that such widely popular magazines as *La Mode de Paris, L'Illustrateur des dames, La Mode universelle,* and *La Mode pour tous* published their first issues. In addition, the development of the modern cosmetics industry during the interwar period created a new focus on beauty and health, and gave rise to lifestyle magazines such as *Votre Beauté* (1932), *Marie Claire* (1937; it reappeared after the war in 1954), *Elle* (1945), and *Femmes d'aujourd'hui* (1950) (Bonvoisin and Maignien 1986).

A few words are needed about the form and content of these new lifestyle magazines in order to fully understand their political function. *Marie Claire* followed the model of the so-called *belle époque* women's magazines, extolling the mainstays of a new feminine aesthetics and hygiene, which had come about through a shift in bourgeois lifestyle in the late nineteenth century (Sullerot 1963). Accelerated industrialization, scientific change, and medical innovations gave rise to a whole new culture of sport, spas, and speculation, which soon preoccupied the bourgeois classes. For women, concepts of aesthetics changed accordingly, bringing with them the sportive, youthful body regulated by a new feminine hygiene based on medical and gynecological progress. Thereafter, one of the functions of women's magazines was to codify a perpetual theme associated with femininity—namely, reproduction—and to educate women on their role as wives, mothers, and caretakers (Smith 1981, 65). The new women's magazines promoted this model of femininity and inscribed the division of the sexes based on sexual difference. As a result, the official register of the press (*guide de la presse*) stopped distinguishing magazines as either "feminine" or "feminist" publications. From then on, women's magazines were subsumed as *journaux féminins* and were defined as having a female readership that constituted more than 60 percent of their total readership (Avrillier, Goyet, and Mingasson 1976, 190).

Following World War II, women's magazines such as *Elle, Femmes d'aujourd'hui,* and the new *Marie Claire* were modeled on the style of their American counterparts to express a newly found societal optimism or *joie de vivre.* In many ways, these publications played a leading role in the state-directed efforts to modernize postwar French society. Ostensibly, they introduced women to the "atomic age but also the age of abundance, of emancipation, of social progress, the age of light, airy houses, of healthy children, of the refrigerator, pasteurized milk, the washing machine, the age of comfort, of quality, and of bargains" (Ross 1995, 84).

Dramatic economic progress and social change helped form this "technocratic society" in postwar France. To this end, the bourgeoisie elaborated myths of progress that promised women more freedoms, but it also created the modern consumer and new forms of conformity. Among the female population, it was homemakers and employees in the tertiary sector who formed the basis of the developing consumer society. Not surprisingly, savvy magazine editors hoped to exploit this emerging market demographic. By informing their readers about products and machines, women's magazines became valued advertising sites in postwar France. Recent scholarship exploring the ideological functions of modern women's magazines points to the discursive construction of gender identities in these publications. In particular, these studies show how women's magazines sometimes juxtapose discourse on gender relations and the division of labor, which can produce ambivalent (if not jarring) ideas of womanhood and femininity (Wadia 1991, 262, 270). So it is not unusual, for instance, to find editorial advice on how to be a good cook for the family juxtaposed in the same issue of a magazine to a report on abortion rights. In turn, an article discussing the abortion campaign may feature a paid advertisement for luxury personal hygiene items such as bath soaps and lotions (Duroi and Wolinski 1979; Weiner 1999).

The most successful lifestyle magazine for women, *Elle,* appeared on the market with impressive credentials. Founded by a well-known woman journalist, Hélène Lazareff, *Elle* was, and still is, read predominantly by middle- and upper-class women in professional households. These groups of women, needless to say, are historically associated with leisure time and disposable income. The magazine soon became known for its optimistic attitude and its excellent use of media technology. After the long years of depression and austerity during the war, *Elle* presented readers with a new world of color, luxury, and opportunity. Like other popular women's magazines, it used a number of tactics to appeal to readers. Underlying the magazines' strategies was what Roland Barthes (1992) called a *gynaeceum,* a women's space that provides a "socially sanctioned structure" in which women are encouraged to consume the images of other women and therefore the commodities that render the models in these images so desirable (Fuss 1992, 721). Barthes and other scholars of popular culture pointed out that this women's space, the fashion magazine, "is widely understood to be a world without men, yet one that is animated by them. Men's conspicuous absence from fashion imagery is in direct relation to their presumed central role in the lives of the female addressee of the magazine: it is for 'his' eyes that the magazines' consumers study the arts of beauty and dress" (Lewis 1997, 94).

As Reina Lewis has demonstrated, however, the argument that popular women's magazines *always* encourage women to look at themselves and at other women the way men do, through what Laura Mulvey (1975) has termed the "male gaze," is not entirely true. Lewis has argued that the "'all female' world of the fashion magazine" also produces a "female gaze" of desiring consumers (1997, 95). However, as she instructs us, the underlying heterosexual rationale of the social institution "women's magazines" (as opposed to "men's magazines"), and the inconsequentiality of fashion itself, renders this potentially subversive viewing position (i.e., the female gaze) powerless "to the point where it is quite clearly not an uncomfortable experience for a heterosexual viewer to gaze at female flesh in this way. She can, after all, imagine that she is looking at them in order to learn how to make herself that desirable for her man" (ibid.). In short, the production of desiring consumers in women's magazines, whether transgressive or not, is driven by the need to satisfy the heteronormative viewpoint, the male gaze, constructed in patriarchal culture (Halberstam 1998; Young 2005). Importantly, as women's magazines successfully evoke readers' desires—for love and sexual pleasure, but also for work, community, and freedom and liberation—these desires "quickly get channeled into a call to purchase the newest sweater, eye makeup, food product, or car. In women's magazines, desire means consumption" (Farrell 1994, 622).

Thus, in reproducing the production of a gendered desire for consumption, women's magazines fail to live up to their promise to provide an "authentic" women's space for their readers. Instead, magazines construct an illusion "that masquerades as pleasure for the female reader" (Farrell 1994, 622). Important for this study, recent research into the reading process of popular magazines suggests that readers can take an active role in negotiating the "preferred" ideological meanings, or even engage in oppositional readings, of such texts (ibid., 623). However, it also suggests that readers' responses to media content "cannot be characterized entirely by either acceptance of or resistance to hegemonic values. . . . There is considerable variation, depending on the nature of the text and the age, social, social class, and ethnicity of the . . . reader" (Crane 1999, 543). Given the sustained popularity of women's magazines over time, it seems that readers' potential to deconstruct, or "decode," the magazines' message does not necessarily cause them to refuse the pleasure these publications offer them. Rather, as Amy Farrell has suggested, these "incongruities" help to explain the lasting attraction of women's magazines (1994, 626; Swingewood 1977).

When the social function of women's magazines is viewed in this light, Barthes's explanation that magazines act as signifying systems that turn items such as fashion, beauty, cooking, housekeeping, and culture into narratives endowed with meanings becomes quite clear (Hazan 1986). A garment depicted in fashion photography, for instance, may signify leisure. One such example is blue jeans. The arbitrariness, or contingency, of such signs, however, becomes masked, or in Barthes's terms "mythologized," in society's effort to make its norms seem like a simple fact of nature. Accordingly, "fashion" enacts its own myth by making the aristocratic model out of which it evolved the source of its current prestige, all the while promoting mass consumerism (Barthes 1983). Barthes's argument provides important clues for understanding how cultures construct their ideas of femininity (just like fashion). It effectively demonstrates that notions of gender are not fixed categories; rather, they are historically specific and continuously shaped and reshaped through social (symbolic) practices. According to Judith Butler (1990), one of these social practices is the self-stylization of the gendered body through which people cultivate distinct ideals of femininity and masculinity. In her pathbreaking study *Gender Trouble,* Butler argues that "gender is the repeated stylization of the body, a set of repeated acts within a highly rigid regulatory frame that congeal over time to produce the appearance of substance, of a natural sort of being" (ibid., 33). Seen in this light, popular women's magazines are one of the sites through which women and men learn how to constitute, or perform, this gendered self-stylization. Arguably, *Elle* participated in this instruction by showing women how to be feminine through an array of advice on beauty, family, and work.

Elle's immediate popularity with female readers undoubtedly stemmed from its eagerness to talk not just about family and reproduction, but also about a comparatively taboo subject: female sexuality. This was done deliberately. Françoise Giroud, the magazine's editor in chief until 1952, explained it in these terms: "The frankness of *Elle*'s tone was, at that time, revolutionary. Remember that before the war, *Marie Claire* would not even allow itself to print the word 'lover.' Women had only husbands or fiancés. Moreover, this freedom has not facilitated the development of the magazine, since entire regions were closed to it. But it made, at the same time, for the magazine's originality and reputation" (1972, 124).

Giroud and Lazareff, the two creators of the magazine, shared a vision about women's new place in society, and they used *Elle* for those purposes. Part of this vision was women's sexual liberation. For instance, Giroud (1972, 127) prided herself on having been the first journalist in France to write about frigidity in a nonspecialized magazine. Interestingly, talk in *Elle* about female sexuality was at times confounded with talk about women's reproductive function and couched in terms of beautification. Fashion advice on skin and hair care, makeup tips for the face (mouth and eyes), and proper vigilance for the belly and breasts, all offered images of femininity that are in fact practical techniques of being female (of having a female body that reproduces the species). Importantly, after coaching women about the outside of their bodies, especially their skin and hair, *Elle* taught them about what is particularly feminine on the inside, namely, the vagina and uterus. In this way, *Elle* drew upon sexual characteristics to talk about women's biological role as mothers. Here it becomes clear how Giroud meant teaching women (through *Elle*) about their own bodies to be a means to better domesticate women's bodies and make them more desirable through consumption. Hence, problematic experiences with women's sexuality—such as frigidity—were likely understood as a symptom of poor choices with regard to consumption, not just of repressed sexuality. If a reader experienced frigidity, this would signal to her that she had failed in properly taking care of her body. Thus even *Elle*'s "revolutionary" feminine world remained anchored in the bourgeois model of the family unit, held together by women's domestic savvy and consumption.

Starting in 1970, however, women activists began to challenge the French government to redress repressive abortion laws and to acknowledge women's reproductive rights. Rather than avoid this crucial issue, *Elle* actually situated itself as an important player in French postwar sexual politics because of its self-proclaimed agenda to further women's sexual liberation. This agenda had marked public consequences. For instance, in 1970, *Elle* instituted the above-referenced "Women's General Assembly" reminiscent of the États-généraux of 1789, which had famously ended absolute monarchy and feudal privileges, and promulgated the declaration of the rights of man and citizen. In preparing for this three-day event, which was held in November 1970 in Versailles (the historic site outside of Paris of the États-généraux in 1789), *Elle* conducted surveys around the country to find out what French women wanted from their political representatives. The results showed that ordinary women wanted the government to legalize the use of contraception and abortion, to institute gender equity in employment, to acknowledge that motherhood contributed positively to society, to make flexible working hours available for mothers, to provide legal equality between wives and husbands, to allow divorce by mutual consent and alimony, and to subsidize maternity and prenatal care—and these demands were presented to the political elite during the event. *Elle* claimed that 1,500 women attended the meetings in Versailles to hear what French women and the invited guest speakers (all of whom were men) had to say about "women's condition" (Mauduit 1988).

However, *Elle*'s genuine effort to create a "real" political space and women's solidarity to rally for women's rights (as opposed to an "imagined" space and sisterhood) through the act of reading and writing was also challenged. For instance, a small group of women activists from the MLF who called themselves "les Petites Marguerites" crashed *Elle*'s press conferences at the "Women's General Assembly" to show that the event was nothing but "hot air" produced by male so-called specialists who catered to the male political elite. During these events, movement activists occupied the microphones at press conferences and presented "mock" questionnaires about important women's issues to the attending journalists, as well as set up information booths outside the halls to talk about abortion rights (Tristan and Pisan 1977, 60–63).

Importantly for our purposes, *Elle* later presented itself as part of this activist movement by referring to the women who derailed and mocked its "Women's General Assembly" as "sisters" (in arms). Furthermore, *Elle* claimed that the fact that the MLF had paid attention to its events and had sabotaged them was a sure sign that the magazine had tapped into an important sociopolitical issue and that its actions had left an essential mark on the radical French women's liberation movement (Mauduit 1988).[4] In so doing, I argue, *Elle* moved from contributing to an "imagined" sisterhood to advocating "real" collective action by women.

Elle's advocacy of feminist activism became particularly visible in the 1970s with its support for the decriminalization of abortion. First, it informed its readers about the state of the abortion law in France. In an article titled "Who Is Guilty?" from October 1972, readers were told about the so-called Bobigny trial outside of Paris, involving four women who were accused of breaking the French law against abortion (see the last section of chap. 1). The coverage of the trial in *Elle* (as well as in other magazines and newspapers) pointed to the grave problems associated with the French prohibition of abortion, as large numbers of French women each year either were obtaining illegal abortions in France or were traveling elsewhere to receive legal medical care (Elle 1995, 230–31). Public coverage of the "Bobigny" trial in *Elle* and other media outlets quickly turned the abortion issue in France into a public policy issue with which the government had to grapple.

Second, *Elle* invited its readers to participate in these public policy debates about women's reproductive rights. An article from 1974, for example, used the upcoming parliamentary debate on a proposed abortion law (the Veil law) to inform readers about the centrality of the French feminist movement to this achievement and to encourage them to engage themselves in the struggle for women's rights (Elle 1995, 238–41). Similarly, a few years later, when the Veil law (now called the Pelletier law) was again up for a vote, *Elle* encouraged its readers in an article to participate in the many street demonstrations that were being organized by the feminist movement to uphold it (Duroi and Wolinski 1979; Tournier 1979). Although there are no records to show how many readers heeded the magazine's call to political action, *Elle*'s decision to support the feminist ideas articulated during this time of social change certainly contributed to the public debates about abortion, which turned some of the ideas advocated by and through the magazine into specific pieces of legislation (such as the Veil and Pelletier laws). It is for this reason that I shall interpret the debates about reproductive rights as an example of the function of *Elle* to mediate changing societal attitudes about women's (and men's) gender roles in postwar French consumer society. And it is to this discussion that I will now turn.

Bodily Self-Fashioning and Reproductive Rights

For pronatalist France, which had historically promoted demographic politics directed at increasing population size, the decriminalization of abortion in 1975 through the Veil law, which was upheld in 1979 through the Pelletier law, marked a veritable sea-change in national reproductive politics. This policy shift was preceded by a new law in 1967, the Neuwirth law, which allowed the use and distribution of contraception in France.

This historical context is important for understanding the political dynamics in the issues of *Elle.* The magazine credited itself with contributing to the public debates on the abortion laws. It did so by providing its readers with information on existing abortion laws, by offering them a way of understanding and engaging with reproductive rights, and by supporting in its coverage the MLF's demands for equal rights. A closer look at *Elle*'s coverage of the abortion issue reveals that of all the articles on women's reproductive rights in the magazine, the most frequent subject was always contraception. Crucially, even after 1985, when pro-life organizations in France started to threaten the abortion law, *Elle* presented more articles on contraception than on abortion. However, as the MLF could demonstrate in its efforts for women's rights, conservative social forces clearly constructed a relationship between contraception and abortion. In *Elle,* at least, the article titles say it all: "He Dares Say: If I Was a Woman I Would Not Take the Pill," "Controversy about Our Survey: French Women Like the Pill Less . . . Five Doctors Respond," or "Does Making Love Give You Cancer? Doctors Respond" (Guichard 1982; Cuisinier 1984; Renaudin and Janneau 1985). These writings demonstrate the centrality of women's bodies to the debate, but even more so the persisting social ambivalence toward women's rights.

Indeed, this ambivalence was of such magnitude that in order to clarify the matter, *Elle* often called upon its most trusted expert: the doctor (and a male one at that). By associating certain health risks with the pill—particularly cancer and vascular diseases—*Elle* represented women's reproductive capacity as a liability, both for the health of each individual woman and for the well-being of society as a whole, since it apparently posed such a threat to fertility. In the same vein, doctors also linked the potential medical dangers of the pill with the "moral dangers" that appeared when women used contraception: that is, an alleged female promiscuity. Many critics had accused women of potential immorality when they tried to block the legalization of abortion. Not surprisingly, then, doctors evoked readers' fears about (illegal) abortions to discredit the pill as a form of birth control: "We have to ask ourselves if the risks [of the pill], which we are beginning to uncover, are equivalent or not to the risks which one would take if the pill would be taken off the market. That is to say, similar to the complications of criminal abortions" (Guichard 1982, 10).

This is an extraordinary passage. This doctor argued that contraception was as dangerous to women as were criminal abortions. Since women could not truly control how they used the pill, it needed to be proscribed by the medical establishment and, by extension, the state. In other words, women could not control their own biological needs. Even more, such statements reduced women to their biological specificity, their individual lifestyle and social conditions notwithstanding. By providing a forum for these kinds of claims from doctors, *Elle* reproduced reductive notions of womanhood based on reproduction—although the magazine made honest efforts to counter this effect. In one article, for instance, *Elle* interviewed Mme Simone Veil, who had been instrumental in writing the abortion law, and quoted her as saying: "Ever since people fought against abortion, there were always those who turned back the clock by making women afraid" (Renaudin and Janneau 1985, 91).

Around 1985, a cluster of articles on reproduction were published to mark the tenth anniversary of the abortion law. Since 1975, *Elle* had published seven articles on abortion, describing primarily women's rights under French law and the main players in the national abortion debate. In 1979, for instance, an article titled "Abortion: The Campaign Is Open" introduced readers to the spokeswomen for some of France's pro-choice organizations and gave information on scheduled street demonstrations organized by the women's liberation movement to challenge the law criminalizing abortion at that time (Duroi and Wolinski 1979). The article also looked at the positions taken by the political parties on abortion. Throughout, we learn where the MLF and its leaders, including Simone de Beauvoir, stood on this issue. The article concluded that laws that criminalize abortion had stopped few women from having one if they were determined (or wealthy) enough, resulting in many unnecessary deaths. (See chap. 1, n. 8, for statistics on abortion deaths in France.)

Another article from the same year, titled "Abortion: A Dossier Black and White," offered readers practical information on how to navigate current abortion policies. First, it updated them on the availability of abortion clinics and other abortion services by region. It also explained, step by step, what women needed to do in order to get an abortion, where they could obtain addresses for hospitals and clinics, and what they could expect to happen in the required counseling sessions (Tournier 1979). Yet in both articles, paid advertisements appear next to the text, seemingly contradicting the empowering messages. In "Abortion: The Campaign Is Open," the text is placed next to an advertisement for shower and bath lotions (Duroi and Wolinski 1979, 121). Similarly, "Abortion: A Dossier Black and White" appears next to an advertisement for Clarins beauty lotion (Tournier 1979, 15).

In articles such as these, *Elle* seems to have clearly conveyed the following message: In the ten years following the new abortion law, women's role in society might have changed considerably, because women had been liberated from involuntary childbearing and the duties of child-rearing. At the same time, however, a woman's feminine identity was still construed as being an object of desire. In fact, in an issue of *Elle* published in June 1980, an article advising readers on how to get reimbursed for an abortion appeared right next to a photo spread featuring the newest line of wristwatches on the market. This example is especially telling, since the watches are not part of a paid advertisement that might have been accidentally placed next to the blurb on reimbursement for abortion. Instead, in combination, the acts of choosing a watch and choosing an abortion provider may both become issues of style (Wolinski 1980).

Of course, the abortion advice in *Elle* examined in the two examples above is open to divergent readings. On the one hand, it can be seen as delivering much-needed information to readers in an important area of women's concerns that the paid advertisement for beauty products placed next to it only seemingly contradicts. Or it could be understood as an instance of "covert advertising," the systematic establishment of links between editorial material and purchased advertising (McCracken 1993; Farrell 1994, 622). Seen in this way, *Elle*'s efforts to support a woman's right to reproductive freedom by giving advice on abortion issues nevertheless remained caught up in the desire/commodity nexus sustained by popular magazines. Distinct ideas about women's rights and women's empowerment developed by feminist activists became commodified by the mass media. However, since we do not know for sure how readers understood the magazine, it is important to point out the occurrence of such competing discourses within the texts despite the possibility of readers' agency (Farrell 1994, 623).

Along with advice on abortion, *Elle* suggests that the availability of RU 486 could replace the need for surgical abortions, which had been at the center of public controversy for so long (Renaudin 1984). However, conservative forces opposing all forms of abortion were so powerful that they initially caused Roussel Uclaf, the chemical company that produced RU 486, to suspend its distribution. In 1988, the socialist government acted decisively and forced the producer to make RU 486 available to women in France. Typical of its avant-garde ambitions, *Elle* tackled the issue with great respect for innovation and warned against any moralizing about the matter. Then, in its usual documentary fashion, the magazine explained how RU 486 was being administered and how its ingredients worked (Renaudin 1984, 1988a, 1988b). Commenting on the new generation of abortive and contraceptive pills (such as the "morning-after pill") that aid women in controlling their bodies, Françoise Tournier writes in a 1988 editorial: "The morning-after pill constitutes scientific progress. Thus, a human progress. . . . We thought that the times of the knitting needle and the parsley stalk were over" (1988, 7).

In ways reminiscent of its 1970 "Women's General Assembly," the magazine even published the views of its employees regarding the issue (Renaudin 1984). By bringing women's personal opinions and accounts into the discussion of the abortion pill, *Elle* made an effort to contest the patriarchal discourse on women's condition. But these articles also opened "the dossier," "the debate," or "the campaign" to bring such clearly demarcated women's issues into the feminine world of consumerism, where subversive feminist ideas about women's empowerment developed by the MLF become commodified. At the same time, I argue, *Elle*'s inclusion of personal opinions and accounts, which make readers' experiences with oppression more real, also contributed to the creation of a shared sense of belonging and "sisterhood" among women. The last cluster of reporting by *Elle* on French sexual politics and women's rights, that is, coverage on threats to the abortion law, can further help to illustrate this point.

Beginning in 1985 and throughout the 1990s, France witnessed a steep increase in organized antiabortion movements. These groups included organizations such as SOS Futures mères, Laissez-les vivre, and Association pour l'Objection de Conscience à toute Participation à l'Avortement (AOCPA) (Allison 1994; Venner 1995). In response to these right-wing threats, in 1993 the Neiertz law made any person's obstruction of the abortion law a crime punishable by prison (from two months to two years with fines). Up to 1998, *Elle* published five articles on the imminent threat to the abortion law. These articles passionately argued for the feminist belief in a woman's right to abortion. In "A Video against Abortion: Images That Create Fear" and "Freedom Threatened," the magazine not only reported on the violent actions by antiabortion groups and the government's response in making any infringement on a woman's right to abortion a crime, but it also discussed the decreasing availability of abortions to women around the country because of clinic closures, increased fees for the procedure, and unwillingness on the part of the medical establishment to act on the law (Andréani, Mareuil, and Corre 1985; Sandrel 1989). Here, *Elle*'s reports drew particular attention to the (mal-) practice of many hospitals in administering abortions up to the eighth week of pregnancy, although the law allows abortions up to the tenth week.[5] Similarly, in the case of the antiabortion commandos, who were tied to the extreme right, *Elle* reported on the groups' background in appealing to readers to remain vigilant for women's rights, for which the women's movement had fought hard, and which had built the foundation for the modern woman to live independently (Sandrel 1989).

On the subject of women's independence, *Elle* is particularly quick-witted in its ability to write the history of the French feminist movement onto its own legacy—and vice versa. In a 1983 "documentation" titled "Feminism Is Dead . . . Long Live the Liberated Woman," the magazine traced the evolution of French second-wave feminism from its inception around 1968 to its alleged end in the 1980s (Clerk 1983). In the article, the women's liberation movement is depicted as having gone through a number of distinct developments, with the goal of making itself superfluous in a postfeminist society in which gender equality has been achieved. As if to illustrate the point that feminism and the feminist movement were "dead" and no longer needed, the same article featured an ad for women's lingerie next to the main text celebrating women's newly found "femininity." The Warner bra ad echoed the slogan of the second-wave feminist movement for a woman's right to control her own body with the caption "Respect the body." The ad went on, however, to state that this bra rivaled no other in its "femininity" ("Respect du corps" 1983).

In this way, the messages of the ad and the text of the article manage to incorporate two seemingly contradictory concepts of womanhood: the liberal ideal, that women are equal to men, and the feminine ideal, which celebrates biological difference from, rather than equality with, men. As we have seen earlier, these two concepts of womanhood, sameness with and difference from men, constitute the "paradox" (Scott 1996, 3) of French feminism and its political struggle for women's rights. In the pages of *Elle*, the subversive nature of feminist discourse, despite its ideological division into opposing groups, or strands, such as "liberal" or "radical" feminisms within the movement, become appropriated and channeled into the desire/consumer nexus as one overarching "feminist" idea that women ought to experience their bodies freely through consumption.

Once again, women's consumerism—with its emphasis on fashion and beauty—is brought into the feminine world of *Elle* through personal accounts and stories. Even clearly demarcated "women's issues," such as abortion and contraception, are personalized in this fashion in order to "soften" the reports and to make women's experiences more valid. In "Abortion: A Dossier Black and White," a rather abstract and analytical feature full of statistics is softened by the personal accounts of four women who had abortions (Tournier 1979). A married woman with a child who was in the process of getting a divorce and found herself pregnant again tells readers how thankful she is that she had recourse to an abortion, as she did not want to have another child with the man who was leaving her. According to her testimony, the procedure was done at a hospital and went unexpectedly well, without any complications, although it left her saddened: "Luckily, the abortion was performed in the hospital (check in the night before, leave the evening of the intervention) without the awkward feeling of former times, with just the right atmosphere of anonymity and understanding. Nothing more. A day without exception, a dull day" (ibid., 9).

From her emphasis on "luck" in not having experienced any medical complications from the abortion, the readers, of course, must assume that medical problems associated with abortions are a matter of bad luck and cannot be helped. This idea is underscored in the second personal story contained in this article, in which a woman shares her experience with a botched abortion: "After the abortion, I am not feeling well. I continue to bleed. I have to see the doctor again: I am told that the egg may have lodged itself outside of my uterus! Did I get an abortion the first time around, or not? I don't understand anything anymore. . . . A friend recommends another doctor. . . . [In the hospital,] I am told that I am still pregnant! Everything is back in order now, but I am exhausted morally and physically" (Tournier 1979, 9).

By portraying the experience of abortion as one in which women lose control over their bodies and can become the victims of an uncertain science, I argue, these stories do more than simply use personal narratives to attract readers. They use the real or potential experiences of abortion and the fears associated with it to create a shared sense of belonging and "sisterhood" among women with the potential to call for political action (Tournier 1979; Soriano 1982). At times, *Elle* used this potential for collective political action (i.e., women's sisterhood) to help with the formulation and to offer support for equal rights demands, which contributed to the creation of distinct pieces of legislation in France in the 1970s, 1980s, and 1990s, most notably the abortion rights acts of 1975 and 1979. While the feminist project for just citizenship rights provided *Elle* with a unique opportunity to address women's needs, the magazine's function to market ideals of femininity to its readers produced ambivalent and even contradictory notions of female subjectivity, which at times seem to bolster and at other times to challenge the feminist endeavor.

If women's popular magazines such as *Elle* conflate politics and consumerism, and if this conflation in some ways undermined feminist goals, I should caution, however, against dismissing these texts as "bad" or "simplistic" materials. Rather, women's magazines offer a world of images and information that readers can relate to their own life experiences and use to build a broader sense of confidence in their beliefs and in their actions. Furthermore, by discussing perceived feminine norms, these magazines help create a common bond or "sisterhood" among women readers, which can become a politically potent basis for women's collective action. Nowhere is this more clear than in *Elle*'s participation in one such collective effort: the fight for abortion rights in Fifth Republic France. During this time, the magazine contributed to the public abortion debate through its continued reporting on French sexual politics in terms of women's individual rights. The magazine thus provided its readers with political information and offered them a way of understanding, coping with, and even engaging with issues and problems that are shared by other women, such as reproductive rights issues.

This does not mean, of course, that one should readily condone how these magazines represent women, because they often remain reactionary in their efforts to promote consumerism over any other social or political practice. Yet it means that by opening "the dossier," "the debate," or "the campaign" in its reporting on women's issues, *Elle* (like similar magazines) contributes to making a social space (imagined and real) for women that allows for self-fashioning as a means to transform society as a whole.

At the same time that women's magazines such as *Elle* were promoting bodily self-fashioning as part of the postwar feminist project, the militant feminist reviews that were created and circulated by the various groups that made up the French women's liberation movement opened a social space for women beyond traditional feminine expectations and consumer culture. In the following chapter, I will examine how the noncommercial feminist press used reading and writing as avenues for social change.

4 Dissident Citizens

ON AUGUST 26, 1970, nine women trespassed at the Tomb of the Unknown Soldier underneath the Arc de Triomphe in Paris, where they laid a wreath in memory of the soldier's unknown wife. (They had chosen this date because it marked the fiftieth anniversary of women's right to vote in the United States.) Although the women were immediately arrested by the police, the media grasped the symbolism of their act. The next day, the newspapers called attention to how the women had violated a major symbol of French nationalism, referring to them as the women's liberation movement (MLF). Arguably, this was the first time that feminists openly intervened in French political life after World War II. These women wanted to challenge the sexual and political inequalities between women and men that persisted in postwar France. They targeted basic reproductive rights, and they made one thing, in particular, their rallying cry: abortion (Tristan and Pisan 1977; Duchen 1986; Picq 1993).

In this chapter, I analyze how the developing women's liberation movement used public writing about reproductive rights as a vehicle for women's collective political action. Feminist reviews, which mushroomed in France between the 1970s and the 1990s as mouthpieces for a plethora of women's groups collectively known as the MLF, illustrate how women used reading and writing to create a social space from which to challenge women's rights discourses. In contrast to popular women's magazines, however, the feminist reviews offered an alternative social space outside of consumer expectations that made women's corporeal difference from men the basis for collective action (Jenson 1987; Milan Women's Bookstore Collective 1990; Zerilli 2005; Sánchez and Sevillano 2006).

In writing about women's rights in a public forum, these extraordinarily rich sources—a total of more than seventy reviews, produced both inside and outside of Paris—revived an earlier tradition of writing as political contestation and distinct citizenship practice. In the process, I argue, female activists cast themselves in the role of "dissident citizens." In crafting political strategies that skillfully wove together formal (lobbying, petitioning) and informal (street protests, feminist writings) practices, they embodied through their activities what Holloway Sparks (1997) has eloquently called "citizenship dissent." In her words, "instead of voting, lobbying, or petitioning, dissident citizens constitute alternative public spaces through practices such as marches, protests, and picket lines; sit-ins, slow-downs, and cleanups; speeches, strikes, and street theater. Dissident citizenship, in other words, encompasses the often creative oppositional practices of citizens who, either by choice or (much more commonly) by forced exclusion from the institutionalized means of opposition, contest current arrangements of power from the margins of the polity" (75). In Sparks's list of "alternative public spaces," we should also include the feminist print media, which served as a springboard for political activism.

The feminist reviews became an important tool in the political struggle for women's reproductive rights for two reasons: first, they informed readers about the controversial issue of reproductive rights; and second, they provided a forum for women to express and debate contested positions on existing abortion laws. In this manner, the feminist print media allowed women to represent themselves in new symbolic ways and to relate their personal experiences to reproductive issues. This political strategy became central to second-wave feminism in France and elsewhere (and, as we have seen in chapter 3, was successfully appropriated by glossy women's magazines such as *Elle*). Throughout, my main point is that the feminist press helped negotiate a social space for women's collective self-representation, from which political collective action could be launched (Farrell 1998). In this way, the reviews illustrate Jane Jenson's finding that "within a given universe of political discourse, only certain kinds of collective identities can be forged; for more to be done, the universe itself must be challenged and changed" (1987, 65).

Seen in this light, the feminist reviews served as discursive sites, or a "communications network," to use Jo Freeman's terminology, where readers could construct and disseminate particular meaning systems or consciousnesses. In her classic theory of the origins of the women's movement, Freeman has explained that "the need for a preexisting communications network or infrastructure within the social base of a movement is a primary prerequisite for 'spontaneous' activity. Masses alone don't form movements, however discontented they may be" (2006, 27). In other words, we must understand what structural factors allow people to become politically conscious, then to organize into groups, and finally to act to effect political change (Rowbotham 1992). In this case, the feminist reviews gave women activists this kind of prerequisite infrastructure, and allowed them to create a new political discourse or consciousness among French women about restrictive abortion laws (Jenson 1987, 64).

Before proceeding with my analysis of how the feminist press confronted reproductive issues and the law about abortion, I shall clarify a few important methodological underpinnings of the study. As with my analysis of the women's magazine *Elle*, I have selected a representative number of feminist publications that existed between 1970 and 1993. My selection includes *Les Cahiers du féminisme; Elles voient rouges; Des Femmes en mouvements* and *Des Femmes en mouvements hebdo; Les Femmes s'entêtent; Histoires d'elles; Mignonnes, allons voir sous la rose; Les Pétroleuses; Remue-ménage; La Revue d'en face; Le Temps des femmes* and *Le Temps des femmes II;* and *Le Torchon brûle,* which are archived at the Bibliothèque nationale de France and the Bibliothèque Marguerite Durand in Paris. The reviews analyzed for this study are "representative" because of their sizable readership and/or their important contribution to women's rights discourse, as they represent the three main strands of the MLF—the Féministes révolutionnaires (liberal feminists), Psych et po (radical feminists), and Lutte des classes (Marxist feminists)—as opposed to publications by women's associations and centers, such as the MFPF, governmental institutions such as the Department of Labor, or academic publications (El Yamani 1998).

In my content analysis of the reviews, I have examined texts and illustrations, but again, I have not done any formal coding. Instead, I scrutinized each review for information about reproductive rights (including information on contraception and abortion) as well as for how it offered itself as a forum for women to exchange information and experiences on these issues. Overall, my analysis suggests that the feminist reviews, like the various other dissident actions organized by the women's liberation movement, constructed the abortion issue in terms of women's individual citizenship rights and thus expressed women's claim of the right to control their own bodies. (The early twentieth-century French birth control movement had pointed to the connection between female corporeality and reproductive rights, but the women's liberation movement, although intertwined with the birth control movement, is separate from it. The best-known activists of the birth control movement remain Nelly

Roussel in France and Margaret Sanger in the United States. Today, however, the movement's idea of "planned parenthood" has become synonymous with reproductive freedom [Accampo 2006].) The movement's strategy to invest the female body with political meaning proved especially powerful, because historically French body politics have been associated with the male body (of the king in old regime France and of "fraternal" citizens in postrevolutionary France) (Outram 1989; Melzer and Norberg 1998). Yet feminists are not of one voice when it comes to the meaning of reproductive freedom.

According to Simone de Beauvoir, for instance, individual autonomy is based on the prevention of maternity rather than the management or planning of it advocated by the birth control movement. Nevertheless, the strategy to advocate reproductive freedom became central to second-wave feminist discourse in France and elsewhere, and was picked up, or echoed, in popular women's magazines of the time. The idea of the "willed pregnancy" (to use Lealle Ruhl's [2002] terminology), then, underlies (liberal) feminist political activism, as well as state laws governing contraception, abortion, and, since the 1980s, assisted reproductive technologies such as in vitro fertilization.

I have divided this chapter into two distinct sections. The first describes the making of the feminist reviews as a political tool of the nascent French women's liberation movement. The second section then analyzes the attempts by the feminist press to define abortion in terms of women's right to control their own bodies, which culminated in the decriminalization of abortion in 1975 and the renewal of this law in 1979.

The Feminist Press and the Making of a New Consciousness

As discussed in the previous chapters, the French government enacted laws prohibiting contraception, birth control advice, and abortion in 1920 and 1923. Those laws, in turn, were based on article 317 of the Penal Code of 1810. The 1920s legislation was passed largely out of geopolitical concerns: from the late eighteenth century onward, the French state had been obsessed with demographic decline, and had tried to institute health and welfare policies to increase population growth (Quinlan 2007). Following World War II, contraception and abortion laws returned to their pre-Vichy status, but were still explicitly intended to control private sexuality by keeping contraception, birth control, and abortion illegal. In the 1960s, the pronatalist political agenda began to conflict with women's interest in controlling their own fertility. As more and more women received postsecondary education and entered careers, they found it important to manage their pregnancies. At this point, a number of social pressure groups, including the MLF, set out to mobilize politically on women's behalf (Allison 1994).

In their political struggle to revise the abortion laws, women's rights activists resurrected the feminist tradition of political writing of earlier times discussed in chapter 1 (Adler 1979; Klejman and Rochefort 1984, 150–51; Pisano 2002, 69). This time around, in the form of feminist reviews, it was characterized by a militant tone and content, a refusal to adhere to traditional layout and division into traditional sections (such as beauty, fashion, family, etc.) associated with women's magazines, and the use of a collective voice of women instead of the expertise of a single editor (Granger and Desbois 1987; El Yamani 1998, 98-99). The reviews were distributed at small kiosks, on street corners, and at meetings and public events, as well as by subscription. However, the reviews were inconsistently organized into issues and volumes, and they often lacked pagination and a table of contents, as they generally appeared in pamphlet form. Due to a lack of financial resources, a poor distribution system, and internal differences within the movement, many of the reviews ceased publication after a few years or even months. (None of the feminist reviews were controlled by the OJD [Office des Justification de la diffusion], the organization in charge of overseeing the publication and distribution of commercial journals in France. For this reason, circulation numbers are often guessed at or are altogether unknown [El Yamani 1998, 92].) The majority of reviews appeared between 1974 and 1979, a period that coincides with the heyday of the abortion controversy; the second peak period was during the mid-1980s, when activists continued to fight for a more inclusive law, including free access to abortion.

Although these reviews seem anarchic and chaotic at times, they served a vital role in feminist politics, using women's writing as a form of political engagement. Indeed, it is important to emphasize that women's writing often precipitated political engagement. In this instance, organized feminism was arguably inspired by an article published in *L'Idiot international* in May 1970 titled "Combat pour la libération de la femme." Signed by Monique Wittig, Gille Wittig, Marcia Rothenburg, and Margaret Stephenson, it called for a new feminist consciousness and political movement. This piece provoked the first protest action at the Arc de Triomphe, which was organized in part by one of the authors, Monique Wittig. Another organizer of this event was the writer Christine Delphy, who, like Wittig, was one of the main activists of the movement and who also wrote for the feminist reviews (Kandel 1979, 61). (The other participants at the Arc de Triomphe were Cathy Bernheim,

Monique Bourroux, Julie Dassin, Emmanuelle de Lesseps, Christiane Rochefort, Janine Sert, Margaret Stephenson, and Anne Zelensky [Deudon 2003, 5].) Most importantly, the article also inspired the surge of women's groups that made up the MLF. It is not surprising, then, that each group launched its own publication in order to inform (and influence) readers about issues related to women's sexuality, contraception, and abortion (Laubier 1990, 73; Zancarini-Fournel 2004, 237).

In October 1970, the first of these distinctly feminist reviews appeared. It was provocatively titled *Le Torchon brûle* (The Burning Dishrag), a direct allusion to the women revolutionaries of the Paris Commune, who were famously accused of burning down the city's monuments (Gullickson 1992). It lasted for only three years and published six issues, or a total of 35,000 copies. Like many other of the feminist reviews, *Le Torchon brûle* was written by a collective of women. These activists rarely had previous experience with publishing, and they had to learn the trade on the fly. Consequently, their meetings were disorganized and tense as the participants tried to divvy up the work and to classify the contributions by genre, such as personal testimonies, reports, and poems (*Le Torchon brûle,* no. 3 [no year]: 24).

After *Le Torchon brûle,* a myriad of feminist reviews appeared on the scene, including those selected for this study. Before internal ideological differences began to erode the movement by the late 1970s and early 1980s, the strand Féministes révolutionnaires and its liberal egalitarian ideas dominated the French postwar women's liberation movement (Collectif 1981; Offen 1988; Picq 1993). The main reviews associated with this group were *Le Temps des femmes* and *Remue-ménage. Le Temps des femmes* started publication in 1978 and continued through 1983. It reached a circulation of about 5,000 copies per issue, but appeared irregularly. Directed by Jeanne Ralite, its editorial collective consisted of about fifteen women, who were also active in a number of labor unions in Paris. *Remue-ménage* started publication in 1979 and disappeared only one year later. It was published on a monthly basis, and each issue reached a circulation of about 3,000 copies. Nicole Canto supervised the editorial collective.

The second strand, the radical feminists of Psych et po, had one leading publication, titled *Des Femmes en mouvements* (*FM*). It was published between 1978 and 1979 and then turned into *Des Femmes en mouvements hebdo,* which ceased publication in 1982. A monthly publication, it reached a circulation of about 150,000 copies per issue, and because of its popularity, it could qualify as a crossover between a women's magazine and a militant press organ (Kandel 1979, 58; El Yamani 1998, 98). Like some of the other reviews, *FM* featured contributions by women activists who later became well-known public figures and/or writers, including Hélène Cixous and Antoinette Fouque, as well as the fashion designer Sonia Rykiel (*Des Femmes en mouvements*, no. 1 [1978]; *Des Femmes en mouvements hebdo*, no. 1 [1979]).

Finally, the strand Lutte des classes, the Marxist feminists, published a review titled *Les Cahiers du féminisme*, which existed from 1975 until the mid-1990s. Its directorship changed a few times over the course of its existence, which is not surprising given its relative longevity. What was most unusual about this publication was that it included articles written and submitted by men, which conflicted with the MLF's general policy of *non-mixité*, or gender segregation (Zancarini-Fournel 2004, 228). Arguably, this policy allowed women to interact with each other without feeling dominated by patriarchal structures and views and to create a collective voice for women's sociopolitical empowerment. Clearly, women activists accorded the feminist press an important role in providing such a women-friendly space that could contribute to a collective identity, or sense of "we," among women.

Learning to Say "We": The Feminist Press Confronts Abortion, 1970–75

One issue that concerned French women at this time particularly, and which had the potential to unite women collectively, was reproductive freedom. Activist Anne Tristan wrote: "Just the idea of the whole masquerade [of clandestine abortions] we were obliged to undertake—the illegality, the search for addresses, for doctors one could trust—repulsed me. A rage overcame me to do something in order to stop this" (Tristan and Pisan 1977, 64).

In 1971, alongside writer Christine Delphy, Tristan addressed the movement's general assembly, hoping to find support among fellow activists for her belief that the abortion question was central to women's oppression and that it could unite women in the struggle for gender equality. A small group of ten to fifteen women started to meet on a regular basis to work on this project. To raise public awareness and support, they thought of publishing a confession by women who had had illegal abortions. From this idea, of course, grew the "manifesto" of women confessing to having had illegal abortions, which was published in the news magazine *Le Nouvel Observateur* on April 5, 1971. The actual text was written for the MLF with the help of Simone de Beauvoir, whose status as a public intellectual and writer encouraged other famous (and not so famous) women to sign the document (Tristan and Pisan 1977, 63–69; see chap. 1, n. 7). The text started out by saying, "One million women abort every year in France. They do it under dangerous conditions because they are condemned to do so clandestinely, although, when performed under medical supervision, this procedure is extremely simple. No one ever mentions these millions of women. I declare that I am one of them. I declare that I have had an abortion" (MLF 1971).

I noted before that the activists who composed the "manifesto" exaggerated the number of illegal abortions in France at that time as "one million" a year. The actual number was around 120,000 a year (Dumont 2002; Bajos et al. 2004; MFPF 2005, 71–75; see chap. 1, n. 8). There are two possible explanations for the activists' use of these inaccurate numbers. They may have tried to include in their account what in statistical analysis is known as "dark figures," an educated guess at the number of unknown and/or unreported cases of illegal abortions, as well as the cases of the many French women who went to England or the Netherlands to have abortions performed there. More likely, the exaggeration reflects an effort to alert the greater public to this pressing social issue by equating big numbers with big problems.

Curiously, in the early stages of the abortion debate, the conservative government accepted the activists' exaggeration when it tried to overcome opposition to taking action on the abortion law from within its own political party as well as from religious groups and other conservative societal forces. In the eyes of the government, which pursued a conservative pronatalist agenda, large numbers of illegal abortions meant not only that women's societal role as bearers of French citizens was compromised, but that women's reproductive health was threatened by the unsafe and unsanitary nature of clandestine abortions. As Jean C. Robinson (2001) has demonstrated in her key study of the abortion debate in Fifth Republic France, the government tried to advance this pronatalist agenda when it imposed strict rules on pregnancy terminations in its first law decriminalizing abortion. As we shall see further below, when the law was overhauled five years later, in 1979, the government tried to use its newly created Women's Office, the Ministère déléguée auprès du Premier ministre à la condition féminine et à la famille (MDCFF), to maintain its conservative political agenda. When pressed by women's rights activists, the head of the Women's Office, Monique Pelletier, connected not women's rights to reproductive freedom but women's health benefits to legalizing abortion in this crucial time for French sexual politics.

This missed opportunity meant that the feminist reviews still had to raise awareness about how the new laws continued to deny women the equal right to control their own bodies. Consequently, with the "manifesto" in mind, the writers encouraged women to submit letters about their experiences with abortions and other reproductive rights issues in order to illustrate women's status as secondary citizens (*Le Temps des femmes,* no. 1 [1978]: 2). The hope was that by including women readers in the writing and editing, the reviews would appeal to women's shared experiences and struggles to establish a collective identity and create a potential political force (Marso 2006, 173).

In sorting through contributions and writing opinions, the editors also treated authorship in unusual ways, often publishing the pieces without an acknowledged author (although contributors sometimes signed personal testimonies with just their first names). There were a number of reasons for this, some personal, some political. For articles and other contributions, the authors may actually have been unknown, or they may have wanted to remain anonymous because of the private experiences they were documenting. But effacing authorship also had a political point. In eliding the writers' names, the editors wanted to criticize the patriarchal system that had pushed women writers to the margins of public and print culture. At the same time, this anonymity could create a collective voice and a sense of shared empowerment. To achieve this effect, the editors repeatedly employed the collective pronoun "nous" ("we" or "us"). In the texts, "we" ("nous") replaced the inclusive "I" (the writer or writers) plus "you" (the reader or readers). Through these means, the editors transposed the militant nature of the publication onto its readers to create an image of women protesting and fighting together (El Yamani 1998, 143).

In the feminist reviews, this linguistic strategy to create a collective womanhood appeared constantly in the early campaign for abortion rights. The whole point was to get women to speak in a collective "we" when discussing abortion. An editorial in *Le Temps des femmes* declared: "We demand the right to control and know our bodies freely; the right to free abortion and contraception; the right to freely choose maternity and to refuse forced sterilization; the right to invent our sexualities" (no. 1 [1978]: 4). The same strategy appeared in *Le Torchon brûle:*

> For two years now, we have organized in order to fight our collective oppression, of which the ban on abortion is just one aspect. . . . The minimum that a society can do is to provide the means to choose and to take on the responsibilities of having a child. One of those means is to have recourse to abortion even in the ideal case of having been informed about contraception, which is far from being the case in France! All the changes that have been suggested to us are nothing but theirs [men's], offered to camouflage our oppression, beginning with the impossibility of controlling our own

> bodies. That's why it is up to us women to find real solutions to our immediate problems at the same time that we are analyzing our oppression. . . . We are 27 million women who are learning to say "WE." (*Le Torchon brûle,* no. 5 [1973]: 20)

By presenting access to abortion as a right of all women ("we") to control their own bodies, women activists could define it as one of the equal citizenship rights still denied to women in France. Furthermore, by presenting reproductive freedom as an issue of shared corporeal experience among all women, activists turned women's personal experiences into political projects and made women's bodies a locus of political activity.

To emphasize this political point, women activists held up signs at protest marches saying "A child if I want it, when I want it" (Un enfant si je veux, quand je veux), which, together with the chant "Our bellies belong to us" (Notre ventre nous appartient), became the slogan of the MLF. Similarly, the feminist reviews repeatedly expressed their belief in a woman's right to control her body when writing about women's sexuality and reproduction: "My body belongs to me," or again, "The right to control one's own body is an inalienable right, still denied to women through social control by institutions such as the church, school, and family" (*Remue-ménage,* no. 2 [1979]: 33; *Mignonnes, allons voir sous la rose,* no. 1 [1979]: 8). In fact, from the outset, activists were clear in their writings that in the first instance, to be a feminist meant to support women's right to control their own bodies. Again, the "manifesto" proclaimed:

> It goes without saying that we [women] don't have the same right as other humans to control our own bodies. Yet our bellies belong to us. Free and legal abortion is not the ultimate goal of the women's struggle. On the contrary, it is but the most elementary exigency, without which the political fight could not even begin. It is vitally important for women to recuperate and reintegrate their bodies. Their condition is unique in human history: they are human beings who even in modern societies do not have the right to control their own bodies. Up to now, only slaves lived under such conditions. (MLF 1971)

While the allusion to the emancipation of slaves from forced work and social control is not new to feminist rhetoric for women's equal rights, this focus on corporeal politics underscores the centrality of reproductive rights issues to the feminist project of equal citizenship rights at this time. It is for this reason that feminists argued that equality for women entailed different political treatment of different (i.e., female and male) bodies, including free and legal access to abortion for women.

The centrality of corporeal difference to the feminist project is further illustrated in the development of the diverse ideological strands within the MLF. The strand Psych et po, in particular, which at one point in the 1970s claimed to stand for the whole of the movement by turning the letters "MLF" into its own trademark, advanced the understanding of women's sexual difference as a sociocultural practice. This stance is exemplified, for instance, in its promotion of a distinct women's writing that is considered different from men's. It is important to note that "difference feminism," as it is sometimes called, questioned the efficacy of the liberal rights discourse evoked by other feminists, but it nevertheless valorized and supported the invention and creation of women's common spaces, both physical and symbolic, to foster a feminist consciousness. (As Claire Duchen informs us in her influential study of feminism in France, "*Psych et Po* remained conspicuously silent about abortion until they published a four-page article about it in 1979" [1986, 59], which acknowledged the importance of the right to abortion for all of the women activists in their political struggle against masculinist culture and law.) The importance of creating women's spaces for the groups that made up the MLF is exemplified not only by the myriad of feminist reviews that flourished throughout the 1970s and 1980s but also by other cultural practices invented by these groups inside and outside France. Those "spaces" included women's conferences, dances, travel groups, and, of course, women's journals and bookstores, through which women's writing and feminist analysis (including the development of academic women's studies) could flourish. This effort expanded female sociability for political purposes in ways that are still recognizable today (Moi 1985; Milan Women's Bookstore Collective 1990; Zerilli 2005).

An integral part of this development was the creation of the women's health movement, which made corporeal difference central in its aim to teach women about female sexuality and reproduction in order to lessen their dependence on the (male) medical establishment, especially in regard to contraception and abortion. At this time, women's groups started to teach other women safe abortion practices outside of doctors' offices with the aid of nurses and physicians who formed the Groupe information santé, or Health Information Group (GIS), and supported the feminist movement (see chap. 1). Importantly, because women's rights activists, including the MLF, but also the family planning association MFPF (the Mouvement français pour le planning familial) and the pressure group for legal contraception and abortion

MLAC (the Mouvement pour la libération de l'avortement et de la contraception), were basically excluded from formal policymaking channels, they resorted to informal channels to seek impact on public policy. These included large street demonstrations and marches in Paris and elsewhere to demand women's right to abortion (Githens and Stetson 1996, 112; Robinson 2001, 93). The two major events in Paris were marches of more than 10,000 participants in April 1974 and of more than 50,000 participants in October 1979.

"Not a Right, but a Sanitary Measure": Revising the Abortion Law, 1975–79

After heated public debates, French lawmakers passed a new abortion law in November 1974, which went into effect in the beginning of 1975. The text reads: "Article 1: The law guarantees respect for all humans from the beginning of life. . . . Article 4, Section I: A pregnant woman in a situation of distress may demand an abortion from a doctor. The abortion can only take place before the end of the tenth week of pregnancy. . . . A woman who demands an abortion . . . must undergo counseling" at an appropriate counseling center (Loi no. 75-17; see chap. 1, n. 9). The campaign for women's rights continued, however, as women activists attacked the weaknesses of the new law. In the ensuing discussion, they complained that the legislation simply skirted the issue of a woman's right to abortion, because it legalized abortions only for women in distress and only up to the tenth gestational week. It thus required a woman to submit to a medical checkup to determine how advanced her pregnancy was, as well as to obtain psychological counseling in order to determine whether or not she had "really" experienced distress. More conspicuously, the law failed to include minors and foreign women. Minors needed their parents' consent for an abortion, and non-French women had to reside in France for at least six months prior to obtaining an abortion. Another failure of the new law was that abortions were still not covered by medical insurance (*sécurité sociale*), so minors and economically disadvantaged women had no medical access to the procedure. Moreover, the law permitted doctors to invoke the "conscience clause" (*clause de conscience*) in order to exempt themselves from having to practice abortion.

In sum, as the reviews pointed out, the 1975 law may have decriminalized abortion, but it did not guarantee abortion as a right. They considered it crucial for readers to understand this failure as a collective problem that affected the entire sisterhood of women. Disappointed activists branded the abortion law "not a right, but a sanitary measure" (*Les Cahiers du féminisme,* no. 12 [1980]: 2). The reviews picked up on this point over and over again. As one described it, the French "right" to abortion "is not *a woman's right,* nor a social responsibility. It is *an aid for people in distress.* The right, as it stands today, implies the moral and intellectual incapacity of women to be pregnant and is not a choice" (ibid.; emphasis in original).

When the abortion law came up for revision in 1979, women's rights activists hoped once more to become involved in the formal policy debates and processes. But again, pressure groups were virtually not included, and attempts by leftist political parties who supported the activists' agenda to amend the law failed in Parliament as well. Most importantly, perhaps, the newly created Women's Office (MDCFF), headed by Monique Pelletier, "did not engage in [women's] rights discourse" (Robinson 2001, 92). Robinson explains:

> Although Pelletier never disavowed the necessity for legal abortion, MDCFF was notably quiet during these public debates. . . . But neither did the MDCFF follow the lead of feminist groups in arguing that abortion was part of a package of rights due to women, although, when pressed, the ministry conceded that the abortion law had proved beneficial to women's health and that the number of cases of infection had diminished considerably. The women's ministry claim that legal abortions promoted women's health in fact moved the onus for promoting the legislation and defending the continuation of the Veil law from the MDCFF to the Ministry of Health. (Ibid.)

For women's groups, the 1979 decision, known as the Pelletier law, was another disappointment. But as in 1975, they were unwilling to give up their cause to fight for women's reproductive rights. Some feminist commentators, however, argued that with a law in place, the women's liberation movement had lost a common cause (*La Revue d'en face,* no. 8 [1980]: 47). As a response to the Pelletier law and the fear of losing political momentum, a substantial number of new feminist reviews appeared, focusing their coverage on a variety of issues related to the abortion law. Those issues included reimbursement of medical costs through social security and legalization of the "abortion pill" RU 486, as well as the threat to abortion services and doctors by antiabortion extremists, which began emerging in the mid-1980s (Venner 1995).

One of the best examples of the feminist reviews' commitment to the language of women's rights, which can be found throughout their existence, I believe, remains their response to the so-called antiabortion commandos (*commandos anti-IVG*) who staged blockades of abortion clinics and threatened the medical personnel who worked at the facilities. One article proclaimed: "Défendre un juste droit!" (Defend a Just Right) (*Les Cahiers du féminisme*, no. 58 [1991]: 6). A headline warned: "Le Droit à l'avortement menacé" (The Right to Abortion in Danger), while another claimed that abortion was "Un Droit à reconquérir sans cesse" (A Right to Be Endlessly Reconquered) (ibid., no. 57 [1991]: 40; ibid., no. 63/64 [1992]: 29). Thus, from the 1980s into the early 1990s, the feminist reviews continued to invoke the language of women's rights in important policy areas to further the legal guarantee of women's reproductive rights.

In their promotion of abortion rights, however, the reviews sometimes perpetuated an inherent ambivalence in the discourse on reproductive freedom. In order to make women understand that they needed laws that guaranteed safe *and* legal abortions, the reviews published numerous stories of women's terrifying experiences with clandestine abortions. In many instances, these harrowing accounts were intended to evoke a sense of collective victimization among readers. In the weekly *Des Femmes en mouvements*, one reader published the following testimony:

> I can't shake the horrible memory of a clandestine abortion, performed on a small, hard bed stained with blood, where I was cut up alive by a hurried and menacing doctor, who threatened me by saying: "Don't scream, people can hear you, don't breathe, don't move." I bit my lip, to keep myself from breathing. Try to imagine being cut on a very sensitive area of your body, without anesthesia, for a half hour without being able to breathe. I remember his eyes behind very thick glasses. The glasses reflected neither sympathy nor hate, but something more profound and frightening. I saw in his eyes the awareness that he had a cruel power over me, a satisfaction with himself and a horror of what he was doing to me. He did not proposition me; he was definitely eager to get me out of there. But there was, nevertheless, in this situation in which we both found ourselves, a vulgar abuse, a violence that I didn't think I could endure. But still, I was there. I endured it. (*Des Femmes en mouvements*, no. 3 [1978]: 65)

Numerous such examples can be found in the reviews, including, for instance, one young woman's account of being raped by her abortionist (*Le Torchon brûle*, no. 2 [no year]: 4).

The choice to reproduce stories about the abortion "butcher" can be traced to the notorious "manifesto," one of the original sparks for feminist activism and public awareness about repressive abortion laws. In that statement, the signatories declared that they had undergone clandestine illegal abortions under dangerous conditions and they hoped that their collective voice would create a shared sense of empowerment among women. In the feminist reviews, women's personal testimony about real (or potential) abortion experiences—and the sense of victimization connected to it—was used in a similar way. Here it was employed to produce a sense of collectivity among readers in order to raise awareness about social injustices that women face, particularly society's persisting ambivalence about women's rights, which is sometimes shared by proabortion and antiabortion rights advocates alike. The reviews thus underlined the feminist position that women needed laws guaranteeing the right to abortion, not just laws that protected them from physical abuse (although they needed those, too).

The campaign to restrict the antiabortion commandos serves as a good example of successful cooperation between "movement feminism" and "state feminism," to use Gill Allwood's (1998) terms. Arguably, since the early 1980s, with the appointment of Yvette Roudy as the new head of the Women's Office (now called the Ministère déléguée auprès du Premier ministre chargé des droits de la femme [MDDF]) by the socialist government of François Mitterand, the feminist commitment to women's rights was reflected in official policy initiatives. Although the Women's Office had little political clout and an even smaller budget, scholars of state feminism in France underline the importance of Roudy's political identification as a feminist (she was also one of the signatories of the "manifesto") for the political changes the government implemented after the abortion reform in 1975–79. Because of Roudy's feminist commitment, women's rights groups became included in policy debates, and the Women's Office adopted the feminist language of women's rights, especially women's control over their own bodies, as equal citizenship rights. Although the reforms did not go as far as activists had hoped, new policies included the reimbursement of abortion fees in 1982, the legalization of RU 486 in 1988, and the criminalization of antiabortion activities in 1993 (the Neiertz law). After Roudy left office in 1986, however, the success of this cooperation between the movement and the state was increasingly due to the persistent pressure of women's groups on the government and the legislature (Reynolds 1987; Mazur 1995; Githens and Stetson 1996; Robinson 2001).

Although we do not know for certain how many of the political changes that the French government implemented were due to the MLF's sustained political engagement between the 1970s and the early 1990s, my analysis shows that the practice of public writing—both personal and avowedly political—was central to the effort to create a feminist political consciousness and women's political collectivity. While they existed, the feminist reviews paved the way for women's collective political agency by providing readers with information about women's issues and by connecting women with one another. Though we have no records to show how many women (and sometimes men) participated in informal and dissident feminist activism after reading feminist publications (or decided to write for one), it seems likely that the reviews broke the social isolation of many women, and that those women may consequently have developed a political consciousness and perhaps engaged in direct political action. In other words, the written words of the feminist reviews gave women a shared sense of community that allowed them to become politically conscious, then to organize collectively, and finally to act for political change in the name of women's rights. It is for this reason that the women's liberation movement and its press organs exemplified a model of citizenship that fostered social movement participation and political solidarity (Siim 2000).

Although "sisterhood" was a potent motivating force, it did not last. Even in the 1970s, the writing was already on the wall. In France, as elsewhere, the radical claims of 1960s activists could not resist atomization as the "me decade" wore on. As one activist stated: "The big feminine us transformed itself into a 'me, I'" (Remy 1990, 105). Others explain the failure of the MLF to act as an effective pressure group on the government in the early stages of the abortion debate with the fact that it lacked a formal structure and leadership (which was intentional) (Allwood and Wadia 2000; Robinson 2001). In addition, in the 1980s and 1990s, a new neofemininity won out over neofeminism, as backlash politics unleashed a new dogmatism about marriage, security, and romanticism. In the 1970s, sustained economic crises helped fuel this reaction, as women were (again) expected to stay home in order to save employment opportunities for men. By the 1990s, most of the French feminist reviews were already extinct. They had been overrun by their commercial counterparts: popular magazines for "emancipated women." These commercial media emphasize commodity consumption because they focus on individual self-improvement and economic success; they self-consciously avoid a culture of politics and social transformation. By contrast, feminist reviews once aspired to provide a free space where women could articulate their concerns and needs. But that space evaporated.

Scholars agree, however, that feminist ideals have persisted in present-day France, as evidenced by the widespread popular support for parity (*parité*), a constitutional amendment that sought to reform the electoral process by increasing the number of female candidates. Instead of a larger women's movement, there emerged several "project-oriented" feminist groups, which continue to work in specific areas to foster women's equality, including immigration, violence, and reproductive rights, and continue to create forms of female sociability (Jardine and Menke 1991; Allwood and Wadia 2000; Célestin, DalMolin, and Courtivron 2003). Feminist activists were able to celebrate a real success in the area of reproductive rights in 2001, when Parliament passed a new abortion law that guarantees a woman's right to abortion (up to week twelve). This new law no longer requires a woman to undergo counseling in order to demand an abortion. Also, women now have the right, up to week seven, to self-administer abortions through the use of RU 486 dispensed by a nurse (MFPF 2005). In this light, the French state can be seen as having acknowledged the feminist agenda of women's rights as a centerpiece of governmental laws and policies, including French family and population politics, which seem to be no longer grounded on mere demographic concerns (Cova 1997). Recent scholarship on "state feminisms" in France (and elsewhere) have demonstrated how the state can become such an advocate—albeit a conflicted one—of women's movement demands (McBride Stetson and Mazur 1995; Mazur 2001, 2005; Lovenduski 2005). This analysis, then, shows how women's public writings can become an avenue for such feminist demands.

CONCLUSION

MY MAIN POINT IN WRITING this study was to show how women's writing has contributed to feminist political contestations that have challenged the abstract concept of citizenship to include women's rights in postwar France. The feminist political contestations I examined are exemplified in the political struggle for reproductive freedom, in which women collectively challenged the French state to abandon its laws criminalizing abortion and to recognize women's rights. As my analysis of three different types of women's writing—elite feminist theory, women's magazines, and feminist reviews—shows, feminist political contestations still produce ambivalent images of women's identity. Throughout this study, one of my main efforts has been to show how the female body is used as a key political site in the production and reproduction of such ambivalent and contradictory images of women's identity in both dominant and feminist discourses.

On the level of elite feminist theory, for instance, Simone de Beauvoir's attitudes toward the female body revealed deep ambivalences, such as her assessment of the female body as a "sick" and "hysterical" abject body that constitutes a handicap for women. I argue, however, that Beauvoir's texts show how contemporaries denigrated and pathologized female sexuality and motherhood by devaluing cultural representations of the female body, and that a key aspect of Beauvoir's literary and philosophical work remained her concern about how women experience their gendered corporeality in patriarchal culture. In her novel *Les Belles images*, for instance, Beauvoir underscored how patriarchal society constructs women as men's "Other," passive, disorderly, and unable to attain political agency, yet continuously performing their prescribed feminine identity. According to Beauvoir, in order for women to attain equality with men and to escape their sexual oppression, they must first become aware of the female body as a primary locus of patriarchal power. On the basis of this consciousness, women must gain material independence from men through remunerated work at the same time that they struggle for political rights.

Beauvoir's focus on the female body as a site of sociopolitical intervention resonated within the larger women's liberation movement in Fifth Republic France. Yet her critique of patriarchal body politics collided with the increased idealization and commodification of the female body found in the booming postwar business of mass culture, specifically women's periodicals. Arguably, women's magazines such as the French *Elle,* with which virtually every woman came into contact, promote bodily self-fashioning as part of the modern feminist project. They view the beautiful body as a liberated body. Like Beauvoir, thus, women's magazines demonstrate a strong tension between political claims and traditional stereotypes, as the beauty and fashion advice they contain not only reproduces idealized standards of female beauty, but in fact equates femininity with consumerism.

The final part of this study examines images of women's bodies and reproductive roles in concrete terms of political activism—in this case, abortion rights—contained in some of the militant feminist reviews that developed during the height of the French women's liberation movement. Available at meetings and kiosks as well as by subscription, these publications enjoyed a unique success with women, despite their limited circulation and short shelf life. As press organs of a larger social movement, they negotiated a social space for women between traditional feminine expectations and the promise of consumer culture. A reading of these reviews reveals women's need for information and expression of the controversial issue of reproductive rights, drawing attention to the female body as the quintessential site of political negotiation. However, like their commercial counterparts, the reviews had to wrestle with the claims of liberal feminism, the desire to represent and speak for all women, as most of them were managed by white, middle-class women from Paris, who equated women's bodily experiences with their own.

I also hope to have shown that women's writing created a sense of communality or "sisterhood" among French women. Despite its intrinsic limitations, this "sisterhood," in turn, contributed to an empowered political activism in Fifth Republic France. Through the act of writing and reading such diverse materials as theoretical feminist texts, women's magazines, and feminist reviews, women could exchange information, experiences, political opinions, and contestations with each other, which enabled them to become conscious of their shared situation in patriarchal society. It directed them to take collective action against the state and to use the state to safeguard their rights. Thus, women fought not only for citizenship rights, but for women's rights—rights based on women's specific needs. In short, with the struggle for reproductive rights, women contested not only the longstanding monopolization of population policies by the French state, but also the meaning of citizenship rights more generally to include women's rights.

The types of "sisterhood" created by these texts differ in important ways. Still, I believe that both the more conservative female *gynaeceum* created by women's magazines and the militant "sisterhood" of the feminist reviews share a unique feature: the potential for women's empowerment in a male-dominated society. While the role of women's magazines often remains that of a "mediator" in times of changing social values, rather than a catalyst in bringing about sociopolitical transformation, these magazines nevertheless provide an important tool for women. They, too, demonstrate the power of the printed word and show how the mere act of reading and writing can contribute to a shared sense of identity among women. Or, put differently, these media exemplify how the acts of writing and reading can be political in a world in which many citizens, not just women, find themselves politically disempowered and without a voice.

While French women's magazines enjoy continued popularity and market growth, the dissident voices of the feminist reviews have practically disappeared. Today, a smaller number of feminist groups and individuals continue their work on a range of gender-related topics, but many of the newer organizations are "mixed" groups, consisting of both women and men. As Gill Allwood and Khursheed Wadia conclude in their study of contemporary French feminism, "[Many of today's feminists] argue that gender relations will not change without men, and that the engagement of men in feminist struggle is no more questionable than the presence of white people in anti-racist struggles. Even the numerous groups who do not admit men—for example Les Nanas Beurs or Les Maries pas Claire—have been keen to stress that while organised along separatist lines, they are far from being anti-men and that their struggle is one that concerns men" (2002, 219).

Judging from this study, then, it seems that French feminism is not gone from the political landscape, but that the collective "sisterhood" associated with the women's liberation movement becomes harder to "imagine." According to Benedict Anderson, who first wrote about the creation of imagined communities in the case of the "nation-state," one of the factors necessary for their development is a shared cultural consciousness among members. As Anderson explained, it was partly the cultural consumption of shared print media that historically fostered national consciousness. And just as it has become something of an international norm for people to organize themselves as a "nation-state" (as the last wave of nationalism witnessed with the transformation of colonial states into independent states), so has feminism become the ideological underpinning for women's efforts to organize collectively into a political "sisterhood." But owing to a number of factors, including an accelerated commodification of feminist ideas and women's issues, the institutionalization of feminism by the state, as well as the general dilemma experienced by liberal feminism to try to speak for all women, it seems that the cultural consciousness so important to the creation and maintenance of a shared "sisterhood" has changed over time. In its stead, we see a different formation of feminist activism in France today, one that, while continuing the historically pertinent critique of abstract universalism, is seeking new ways to speak and act politically (Allwood and Wadia 2009).

In addition to the proliferation of smaller feminist groups, another recent example of this effort is the parity law of 1999, which demands numerical equality between women and men in the electoral process by requiring political parties to ensure that women constitute 50 percent of their electoral lists. At the heart of the parity debate was the question of whether or not it could produce a more representative (i.e., inclusive) political system. As Scott (2005, 2, 4) has shown, parity advocates argued that the basis of republican citizenship, namely, abstract universalism, ought to include, not exclude, sex (difference) in order to ensure real equality. For this reason, parity advocates promoted women's participation in political government, particularly regarding representation of "women's issues." Opponents also supported the need to increase women's representation in governing bodies, but argued against a measure that would base changes to the representational system on people's intrinsic differences (i.e., sex). What is crucial about this debate for the present study is that both sides agreed that although the republican tradition may be gender-biased, it did produce a representational system that allowed political expression of difference in fact (Allwood and Wadia 2000, chap. 8).

As I hope to have shown in this study, postwar French feminism was instrumental in expressing one of these differences: women's sexual difference from men and the articulation of women's needs stemming from that difference. Crucially, feminist political contestations, alongside contestations by other social movements, have contributed to what Amy G. Mazur (2005) has called a "new model" of feminist public policymaking in Fifth

Republic France, which includes institutionalized channels of feminist advocacy for gender equality.

This important change to the republican policy model can be illustrated, I believe, in the way in which the national symbol of the republic, "Marianne," has changed through time. These transformations and stylizations of the French icon of national "unity" demonstrate the continuing difficulties in overcoming the real differences, particularities, and political cleavages that divide French citizens today—powerful distinctions of class, sex, sexual identity, race, ethnicity, and religion. Importantly, I believe, the many transformations of "Marianne" well illustrate the issues of embodiment related to the gendering of citizenship rights analyzed in this study.[1]

Originally, "Marianne" came to life by governmental decree in 1792 to embody the new republic's freedom and pride.[2] The choice of a woman to represent French democracy was not completely new, however, as "Marianne's" headpiece, the Phrygian cap, had commonly been worn by former slaves of the Roman Empire. Thus, by the time of the French Revolution, sculptures and paintings began to use a female figure wearing the Phrygian cap of the *sans-culottes* to represent the revolutionary values of liberty, equality, and fraternity. Depicted in this way, with a determined look on her face and a pikestaff in her hand, "Marianne" was made to look like a warrior defending the universal republican values—despite her *particular* identity as a woman. As historian Maurice Agulhon explains, the republican values and the myth of national unity thus became embodied in the figure of "Marianne." It is for this reason that she is commonly portrayed in the form of a bust or, as in the famous representation from 1830 by Eugène Delacroix titled *Liberty Leading the People,* as showing off her bare breasts in protest against counterrevolutionary forces (Agulhon 1979, 1989, 2001).

Perhaps the most famous inspiration for "Marianne" remains the 1950s actress and sex symbol Brigitte Bardot, who made "Marianne" a symbol of upper-class French-ness rather than the lowly laborer previously associated with her. More recently, "Marianne" featured prominently as part of the bicentennial celebrations of the French Revolution in 1989, when the postal service reissued a stamp in her honor. Additional new models for "Marianne" were selected in 1999, 2002, and 2003, as she now represents a republic that recently adopted a constitutional change to promote parity between female and male political candidates in the electoral process and a republic that is more mixed (*plus mélangée*), or diverse. In the meantime, "Marianne's" image has been plastered on letters, books, and trinkets across the nation and reproduced a million times on stamps and other household products, which commodified her as *the* French cultural icon. Walter Benjamin (2000), who commented on the commodification process of modern politics in his studies on media culture, famously described this development as the politics of art. In this way, "Marianne," and the media spectacle of selecting her, functions to represent the republican effort to incorporate differences based on sex, race, class, ethnicity, sexual orientation, and religion into its abstract concept of citizenship, which, as we have seen, has been sometimes more and sometimes less successfully challenged by women and other new and forceful political actors (Martel 1999).

Even as women enter French public culture and politics in greater numbers and become more accepted as equal citizens, women's bodies remain an important site of political struggle. I hope to have shown in this study how postwar women's rights activists successfully appropriated disembodied liberal citizenship rights discourses to make the female body a key political site in their struggle for abortion rights beginning in the late 1960s. One particular strategy that they used in their political contestations was the creation of "real" and "imagined" sisterhoods through the act of reading and writing about women's corporeal experiences with sexuality and reproduction.

Throughout this period, women's political enterprise was confronted with the promise of consumer culture to channel, if not resolve, women's experience with sociopolitical inequalities into commodity fetishism that potentially undermines women's political mobilization. An example of these processes is the world of popular women's magazines, which all too often conflates politics with consumption.

As for the abortion rights campaign, activists in postwar France could witness, however, that even mass cultural texts, such as for-profit women's magazines, can contribute to the creation of a female identity, or consciousness, with far-reaching political potential. While women's rights activists were not satisfied with the outcome of their lobbying efforts in the 1970s that led to the decriminalization of the French abortion law, their continued focus on women's rights discourse demonstrates that in France, issues of women's embodiment are central to raising awareness about social justice, including women's equality.

NOTES

INTRODUCTION

1. As Jane Abray informs us, the term "feminism" (*féminisme*) did not come into use in French until the nineteenth century. Coined by the socialist Charles Fourier in his *Théories des quatre mouvements et des destinés générales* ([1841] 1967), it was taken up by the French feminist Hubertine Auclert to denote the modern concept of a social movement working for women's emancipation (Abray 1975; Offen 1994, 157).

2. For feminist critiques of the public/private divide, see, for instance, Eisenstein 1981; Elshtain 1981; Pateman 1987, 1988; Kerber 1988; Landes 1988, 1998; Ackelsberg and Shanley 1998.

3. Jo Freeman (2006) and Anne M. Valk (2008) have examined how inherent differences have influenced the women's liberation movements in the United States. For feminist critiques of the liberal concept of "sisterhood" that leaves differences of race, class, ethnicity, sexual identity, age, and other factors unchallenged, see, for instance, Diamond and Quinby 1984; Lorde 1984; Young 1990; Lyshaug 2006; McDonald 2006; Valk 2008; Ackelsberg 2009.

CHAPTER 1. *The Body, Writing, and Citizenship Rights*

1. In an exception, female members of the royal court were actively participating in political life in the sixteenth and seventeenth centuries, but their role was severely curtailed by the end of the seventeenth century (Hufton 1992).

2. Studies on the role of gender and women's political activism in revolutionary France include, for instance, Applewhite and Levy 1984; Fauré 1985; Godineau 1988, 1990; Landes 1988; Rosa 1988; Marand-Fouquet 1989; Soprani 1989; Levy and Applewhite 1990, 1992; Offen 1990; Hufton 1992; Hunt 1992; Melzer and Rabine 1992; and Riot-Sarcey 1995.

3. Around the time of the Revolution, only 65 percent of women could write their own names (Hufton 1992, xxiii).

4. "Chacun a droit au respect de son corps," Art. 16-1 *Code civil,* Loi no. 94-653 1994-07-29, July 29, 1994. The law can be accessed at http://www.legifrance.gouv.fr/affichTexte.do?cidTexte=JORFTEXT000000549619&fastPos=2&fastReqId=1979052065&categorieLien=id&oldAction=rechTexte. Unless otherwise noted, all translations are mine.

5. It was for this reason that republicans later established secular or state secondary schools for girls to contest the influence of the Catholic Church over women's education (Clark 1984).

6. Since the 1860s, fertility had been measured in number of females of childbearing age. Also since the mid-nineteenth century, pronatalist rhetoric had pointed to moral decay as the cause of depopulation (Roberts 1994; Accampo, Fuchs, and Stewart 1995; M. L. Stewart 2001).

7. The text of the manifesto appeared in *Le Nouvel Observateur* on April 5, 1971, titled "Je me suis fait avorter" ("I had an abortion"), and was signed "Mouvement de Libération des Femmes." The "manifesto" is better known as the "Manifesto of the 343 Whores," but the word "whores" (*salopes*) was not used in the original title of the text. Instead, it was used a week later by a satirical newspaper, *Charlie Hebdo,* with the intention of poking fun at the politicians who now had to deal with this issue (Yan Gilbert, *Le Nouvel Observateur,* e-mail exchange with author, May 27, 2008). The list included such well-known writers as Colette Audry, Christine Delphy, Catherine Deudon, Marguerite Duras, Françoise d'Eaubonne, Annie Leclerc, Violette Leduc, Emmanuelle de Lesseps, Christiane Rochefort, Françoise Sagan, Monique Wittig, and Annie Zelensky. It also included the future politicians Monique Pelletier and Yvette Roudy, as well as lawyer Gisèle Halimi, psychoanalyst Antoinette Fouque, and actresses Catherine Deneuve and Jeanne Moreau. MLF, "Je me suis fait avorter," April 5, 1971, http://tempsreel.nouvelobs.com/actualites/societe/20071127.OBS7018/le_manifeste_des_343_salopes_paru_dans_le_nouvel_obs_en.html (accessed January 31, 2010).

8. The number of abortion-related deaths in France dropped to twenty-nine in 1973 and twenty-six in 1974, and continued to drop after decriminalization in 1975 (to about fifteen deaths per year). While the actual number of abortions increased after decriminalization in 1975, the number of legal abortions has been steady since then at about 230,000 a year, or 30 percent of pregnancies. Despite the actual increase in abortions since 1975, the fertility rate of French women remained somewhat stable at around 1.9 children on average.

9. "Loi relative à l'interruption volontaire de la grossesse," Loi no. 75-17, January 17, 1975. The law can be accessed at http://www.legifrance.gouv.fr/affichTexte.do?cidTexte=JORFTEXT000000700230&fastPos=1&fastReqId=483607414&categorieLien=id&oldAction=rechTexte.

CHAPTER 2. *Secondary Citizens*

1. For an account of the development of the novel as a female genre that produced oppositional sociopolitical views, see, for instance, DeJean 1991 and Auerbach 1978.

For an account of what it means to be a woman writer in post-1968 France, see, for instance, Jardine and Menke 1991.

2. For an insightful analysis of the development of "expert advice for women," see Ehrenreich and English 1978; Hulbert 2003.

3. For a first-rate linguistic study of *Les Belles images* see, for instance, Holland 1988–89; Tidd 2005; and Corbí Saéz 2008–2009. Corbí Saéz echoes Fishwick's analysis of Beauvoir's description of the "abject" female body.

4. The equation of woman with overconsumption is not new in French literature. See, for instance, Zola (1883) 1980; Flaubert (1896) 1995; Triolet 1959.

5. In *The Capture of Speech* (1998), Michel de Certeau explains how the social protest movements of the 1960s and 1970s used language as a tactic to fight social injustices. In chapter 4, I will analyze how the MLF used feminist reviews to disseminate information about women's reproductive rights, for instance, as a way to engender a collective feminist consciousness to further collective political action.

6. Recent scholarship on the cultural construction of eating disorders echoes Beauvoir's forceful analysis of female corporeality in modern consumer cultures. See, for instance, Patterson 1989; Bordo 1993; and Pipher 1997, as well as Woliver 2002 on the pressure experienced by women to not only attain perfect bodies but also produce perfect babies.

7. I would like to thank Yolanda A. Patterson for making me aware of this connection.

CHAPTER 3. *Citizen Consumers*

1. Department stores, which date back to the early nineteenth century, are another example of the creation of a shared female space, as they provide women with meeting places and advice on how to dress, furnish one's home, and spend one's leisure time. See, for instance, Miller 1981; Williams 1982; Bowlby 1985.

2. OJD (Office de Justification de la diffusion), 2008, http://www.ojd.com (accessed January 25, 2010).

3. The mission statement of the foundation declares: "To support the advancement and the role of women in our society and promote women's emancipation through education, vocational training and information." La Fondation d'entreprise ELLE, http://www.ellefondation.net/pags/index.php (accessed November 4, 2007).

4. The success of *Elle*'s tactic to "join" the MLF is also mirrored in its rising circulation numbers following the years of the "Women's General Assembly" in 1970. While its circulation decreased between 1966 and 1970 (from close to 600,000 copies to about 550,000), the number rose again after 1970. By 1973, however, French women's magazines experienced a general decline in readership. *Elle*'s numbers fell to around 300,000 copies in 1976, where they leveled off (in 2006, the French *Elle* published around 350,000 copies) (Bonvoisin and Maignien 1986).

5. The 1975/1979 abortion law covers abortions up to the tenth week of pregnancy, which is twelve weeks after the woman's last period. Hospitals, however, often count not ten weeks of pregnancy but ten weeks without a period, which technically amounts to only eight weeks of pregnancy. Since its revision in 2001, the law

guarantees a woman's right to abortion up to the twelfth week of pregnancy. Also, French women now have the right to self-administer abortions through the use of RU 486 dispensed by a nurse (up to the seventh week). Loi no. 2001-588 2001-7-4, July 4, 2001. The law can be accessed at http://www.legifrance.gouv.fr/affichTexte.do?cidTexte=JORFTEXT000000222631&fastPos=2&fastReqId=496271365&categorieLien=id&oldAction=rechTexte.

CONCLUSION

1. A case in point is the French government's decision in the spring of 2004 to ban head scarves from public schools, as they are seen to introduce religious and cultural differences and undermine the division of state and church and the 2009/2010 debate about banning body veils in public institutions. See H. Asiter, "The Deep Roots of French Secularism," *BBC News Online,* December 18, 2003, http://news.bbc.co.uk/go/pr/fr/-/1/hi/world/europe/3325285.stm (accessed April 22, 2004); and "Vers une loi interdissant le voile integral dans les services publics?" *Libération,* January 22, 2010, http://www.liberation.fr/societe/0101615195-vers-une-loi-interdisant-le-voile-integral-dans-les-services-publics (accessed January 28, 2010).

2. The history of "Marianne" is available to French citizens on the prime minister's website: "Marianne and the Motto of the Republic," June 29, 2004, http://www.archives.premier-ministre.gouv.fr/villepin/en/acteurs/symbols_of_the_republic_185/marianne_and_the_motto_50225.html (accessed September 9, 2010).

BIBLIOGRAPHY

PRIMARY LITERATURE

Les Cahiers du féminisme
Elle
Elles voient rouge
Des Femmes en mouvements
Des Femmes en mouvements hebdo
L'Idiot international
L'Information des femmes
Libération
Mignonnes, allons voir sous la rose
Les Nouvelles féministes
Pénélope
Remue-ménage
La Revue d'en face
Le Temps des femmes
Le Torchon brûle

SECONDARY LITERATURE

Abray, Jane. 1975. "Feminism in the French Revolution." *American Historical Review* 80, no. 1 (February): 43–62.

Accampo, Elinor A. 2003. "The Gendered Nature of Contraception in France: Neo-Malthusianism, 1900–1920." *Journal of Interdisciplinary History* 34, no. 2: 235–62.

———. 2006. *Blessed Motherhood, Bitter Fruit: Nelly Roussel and the Politics of Female Pain in Third Republic France.* Baltimore: Johns Hopkins University Press.

Accampo, Elinor A., Rachel G. Fuchs, and Mary L. Stewart. 1995. *Gender and the Politics of Social Reform in France, 1870–1914.* Baltimore: Johns Hopkins University Press.

Ackelsberg, Martha. 2009. *Resisting Citizenship: Feminist Essays on Politics, Community and Democracy.* New York: Taylor and Francis.

Ackelsberg, Martha, and Mary L. Shanley. 1998. "Private, Publicity, and Power: A Feminist Rethinking of the Public-Private Distinction." In *Revisioning the Political: Feminist Reconstructions of Traditional Concepts in Western Political Theory,* edited by Nancy J. Hirschmann and Christine Di Stefano. Boulder, CO: Westview Press.

Adkins, Lisa, and Diana Leonard, eds. 1996. *Sex in Question: French Materialist Feminism*. London: Taylor and Francis.

Adler, Laure. 1979. *À l'aube du féminisme: Les premières journalistes, 1830–1850*. Paris: Payot.

Agacinski, Sylviane. 1998. "L'Universel masculin ou la femme effacée." *Le Débat*, no. 100 (May–August): 149–57.

Agulhon, Maurice. 1979. *Marianne au combat: L'imagerie et la symbolique républicaines de 1789 à 1880*. Paris: Flammarion.

———. 1989. *Marianne au pouvoir: L'imagerie et la symbolique républicaines 1880 à 1914*. Paris: Flammarion.

———. 2001. *Les métamorphoses de Marianne: L'Imagerie et la symbolique républicaines de 1914 à nos jours*. Paris: Flammarion.

Albistur, Maïté, and Daniel Armogathe. 1977. *Histoire du féminisme français: Du moyen âge à nos jours*. Paris: des femmes.

Allison, Maggie. 1994. "The Right to Choose: Abortion in France." *Parliamentary Affairs* 17, no. 2 (April): 222–38.

Allwood, Gill. 1998. *French Feminism: Gender and Violence in Contemporary Theory*. London: UCL Press.

Allwood, Gill, and Khursheed Wadia. 2000. *Women and Politics in France, 1958–2000*. London: Routledge.

———. 2002. "French Feminism: National and International Perspectives." *Modern & Contemporary France* 10, no. 2 (May): 211–23.

———. 2009. *Gender and Policy in France*. Basingstoke, UK: Palgrave Macmillan.

Anderson, Benedict. 1983. *Imagined Communities: Reflections on the Origin and Spread of Nationalism*. London: Verso.

Andréani, Ghislaine, Stéphanie de Mareuil, and Cécile Corre. 1985. "Une video contre l'avortement: Des images pour faire peur." *Elle*, no. 2079 (November 11): 86–89.

Applewhite, Harriet B., and Darline Gay Levy. 1984. "Women, Democracy, and Revolution in Paris, 1789–1794." In *French Women and the Age of Enlightenment*, edited by Samia I. Spencer. Bloomington: Indiana University Press.

Arendt, Hannah. 1972. *Crisis of the Republic*. New York: Harcourt and Brace.

Arp, Kristina. 1995. "Beauvoir's Concept of Bodily Alienation." In *Feminist Interpretations of Simone de Beauvoir*, edited by Margaret A. Simons. University Park: Pennsylvania State University Press.

Association Choisir. 1975. *Abortion: The Bobigny Affair, a Law on Trial—A Complete Record of the Pleadings at the Court of Bobigny, 8 November 1972*. Translated by Beryl Henderson. Introduction by Simone de Beauvoir. Sydney: Wild & Woolley. Originally published in French as *Avortement: Une loi en procès: L'affaire de Bobigny* (Paris: Gallimard, 1973).

Auerbach, Nina. 1978. *Communities of Women: An Idea in Fiction*. Cambridge, MA: Harvard University Press.

Avrillier, R., G. Goyet, and D. Mingasson. 1976. *Mode d'habitat et rôle de la femme dans la presse féminine et la presse de la maison*. Grenoble: Université des sciences sociales de Grenoble.

Bair, Deirdre. 1986. "Simone de Beauvoir: Politics, Language, and Feminist Identity." *Yale French Studies* 72: 149–62.

———. 1990. *Simone de Beauvoir: A Biography.* New York: Summit Books.

Bajos, Nathalie, Caroline Moreau, Henri Leridon, and Michèle Ferrand. 2004. "Why Has the Number of Abortions Not Declined in France over the Past 30 Years?" *Population & Societies*, no. 407: 1–4.

Ball, Terence, James Farr, and Russell L. Hanson. 1989. *Political Innovation and Conceptual Change.* Cambridge, UK: Cambridge University Press.

Ballaster, Rosalind. 1991. *Women's Worlds: Ideology, Femininity and the Woman's Magazine.* Basingstoke, UK: Macmillan.

Barber, Benjamin. 1984. *Strong Democracy: Participatory Politics for a New Age.* Berkeley: University of California Press.

Bard, Christine. 1995. *Les Filles de Marianne: Histoire des féminismes, 1914–1940.* Paris: Fayard.

———. 2001. *Les Femmes dans la société française au XXè siècle.* Paris: Armans Colin.

Bard, Christine, Christian Baudelot, and Janine Mossuz-Lavau. 2004. *Quand les femmes s'en mêlent: Genre et pouvoir.* Paris: La Martinière.

Barthes, Roland. 1983. *The Fashion System.* Translated by Matthew Ward and Richard Howard. Berkeley: University of California Press. Originally published in French as *Système de la mode* (Paris: Éditions du Seuil, 1967).

———. 1992. *Mythologies.* New York: Noonday Press. Originally published in French as *Mythologies* (Paris: Éditions du Seuil, 1957).

Batiot, Anne. 1986. "Radical Democracy and Feminist Discourse: The Case of France." In *The New Women's Movement: Feminism and Political Power in Europe and the USA,* edited by Drude Dahlerup. London: Sage Publications.

Beauvoir, Simone de. 1949. *Le Deuxième sexe.* Paris: Gallimard.

———. 1966. *Les Belles images.* Paris: Gallimard.

———. 1968. *Les Belles Images.* Translated by Patrick O'Brian. New York: Putnam.

———. 1992a. *The Prime of Life: The Autobiography of Simone de Beauvoir.* Translated by Peter Green. New York: Paragon House. Originally published in French as *La Force d l'âge* (Paris: Gallimard, 1960).

———. 1992b. *Force of Circumstance: The Autobiography of Simone de Beauvoir. Volume 1. After the War, 1944–1952.* Translated by Richard Howard. New York: Paragon House. Originally published in French as *La Force des choses* (Paris: Gallimard, 1963).

———. 2004. *Philosophical Writings.* Edited by Margaret A. Simons with Marybeth Timmermann and Mary Beth Mader. Urbana: University of Illinois Press.

———. 2009. *The Second Sex.* Translated by Constance Borde and Sheila Malovany-Chevallier. London: Jonathan Cape.

Benhabib, Seyla. 1992. *Situating the Self: Gender, Community and Postmodernism in Contemporary Ethics.* Cambridge, UK: Polity Press.

Benjamin, Walter. 2000. "The Work of Art in the Age of Mechanical Reproduction." In *The Continental Aesthetics Reader,* edited by Clive Cazeaux. London: Routledge.

Berlant, Lauren. 1997. *The Queen of America Goes to Washington City.* Durham, NC: Duke University Press.

Bonvoisin, Samra-Martine, and Michèle Maignien, 1986. *La Presse féminine.* Paris: Presses Universitaires de France.

Bordo, Susan. 1993. *Unbearable Weight: Feminism, Western Culture, and the Body.* Berkeley: University of California Press.

Bourdieu, Pierre. 1984. *Distinction: A Social Critique of the Judgment of Taste.* Translated by Richard Nice. Cambridge, MA: Harvard University Press. Originally published in French as *La Distinction: Critique sociale du jugement* (Paris: Éditions de Minuit, 1979).

Bowlby, R. 1985. *Just Looking: Consumer Culture in Dreiser, Gissing and Zola.* London: Methuen.

Brosman, Catharine Savage. 1991. *Simone de Beauvoir Revisited.* Boston: Twayne Publishers.

Bullier, Jacqueline. 1965. "Arts et techniques de la presse féminine." *La Pensée* 124 (November/December): 30–42.

Butler, Judith. 1990. *Gender Trouble: Feminism and the Subversion of Identity.* New York: Routledge.

———. 1992. "Gendering the Body: Beauvoir's Philosophical Contributions." In *Women, Knowledge, and Reality: Explorations in Feminist Philosophy,* edited by Ann Garry and Marilyn Pearsall. New York: Routledge.

Canning, Kathleen. 1999. "The Body as Method? Reflections on the Place of the Body in Gender History." *Gender & History* 11, no. 3 (November): 499–513.

Cantor, Muriel G. 1987. "Popular Culture and the Portrayal of Women: Content and Control." In *Analyzing Gender: A Handbook of Social Science Research,* edited by Beth B. Hess and Myra Marx Ferree. Newbury Park, CA: Sage.

Carretier, Marie-Pierre. 1983. "Les femmes du président." *Elle,* no. 1983 (February 28): 86–89.

Célestin, Roger, Elaine DalMolin, and Isabelle de Courtivron, eds. 2003. *Beyond French Feminisms: Debates on Women, Politics, and Culture in France, 1981–2001.* London: Palgrave Macmillan.

Certeau, Michel de. 1984. *The Practice of Everyday Life.* Translated by Steven Randall. Berkeley: University of California Press. Originally published in French as Volume 1 of *L'Invention du Quotidien: Arts de faire* (Paris: Gallimard, 1980).

———. 1998. *The Capture of Speech and Other Political Writings.* Edited and with an introduction by Luce Giard; translated and with an afterword by Tom Conley. Minneapolis: University of Minnesota Press. Originally published in French as *La Prise de parole, et autres écrits politiques* (Paris: Éditions du Seuil, 1994).

Charzat, Gisèle. 1972. *Les Françaises sont-elles des citoyennes?* Paris: Denoël.

Childs, Sarah, and Mona Lena Krook. 2006. "Gender and Politics: The State of the Art." *Politics* 26, no. 1: 18–28.

Chisholm, Ann. 2001. "Acrobats, Contortionists, and Cute Children: The Promise and Perversity of U.S. Women's Gymnastics." *Signs: Journal of Women in Culture and Society* 27, no 2: 415–50.

Clark, Linda L. 1984. *Schooling the Daughters of Marianne: Textbooks and the Socialization of Girls in Modern French Primary Schools.* Albany: State University of New York Press.

Clerk, Loly. 1983. "Le féminisme est mort . . . vivre la femme liberée!" *Elle,* no. 1946 (April 25): 3–12.

Collectif. 1981. *Chroniques d'une imposture: Du mouvement de libération des femmes à une marque commerciale.* Introduction by Simone de Beauvoir. Paris: Association mouvement pour les luttes féministes.

Colombani, Marie-Françoise, and Michèle Fitoussi. 2005. *Elle, 1945–2005: Une histoire des femmes.* Paris: Fillipacchi.

Conner, Susan P. 1984. "Women and Politics." In *French Women and the Age of Enlightenment,* edited by Samia I. Spencer. Bloomington: Indiana University Press.

Constant, Benjamin. (1818) 1980. *De la liberté chez les modernes: Écrits politiques.* Paris: Poche.

Coole, Diana H. 1988. *Women in Political Theory: From Ancient Misogyny to Contemporary Feminism.* Princeton, NJ: Princeton University Press.

———. 1994. "Women, Gender and Contract: Feminist Interpretations." In *The Social Contract from Hobbes to Rawls,* edited by David Boucher and Paul J. Kelley. New York: Routledge.

Corbí Saéz, María Isabel. 2008–2009. "*Les Belles Images:* Annonciatrices de la rupture du discours maître." *Simone de Beauvoir Studies* 25: 20–29.

Corre, Cécile. 1986. "Téléphone rose: Érotisme tu parles." *Elle,* no. 2095 (March 3): 74–75.

Cova, Anne. 1997. *Maternité et droits des femmes en France, XIXe–XXe siècles.* Paris: Anthropos.

Cowan, Ruth Schwartz. 1983. *More Work for Mother: The Ironies of Household Technology from the Open Hearth to the Microwave.* New York: Basic Books.

Crane, Diana. 1999. "Gender and Hegemony in Fashion Magazines: Women's Interpretation of Fashion Photographs." *Sociological Quarterly* 40, no. 4: 541–63.

Cross, Marcia F. 2000. "Women and Politics." In *Women in Contemporary France,* edited by Abigail Gregory and Ursula Tidd. Oxford, UK: Berg.

Cuisinier, M. 1984. "Polémique autour notre sondage: Les Françaises aiment moins la pilule . . . Cinq médecins répondent." *Elle,* no. 1989 (February 20): 42–45.

Curthoys, Ann. 2000. "Adventures of Feminism: Simone de Beauvoir's Autobiographies, Women's Liberation, and Self-Fashioning." *Feminist Review* 64: 3–18.

Dardigna, Anne-Marie. 1979. *La Presse "féminine": Fonction idéologique.* Paris: François Maspero.

DeJean, Joan. 1991. *Tender Geographies: Women and the Origins of the Novel in France.* New York: Columbia University Press.

DeJean, Joan, and Nancy K. Miller. 1991. *Displacements: Women, Tradition, Literatures in French.* Baltimore: Johns Hopkins University Press.

Delphy, Christine. 1984. *Close to Home: A Materialist Analysis of Women's Oppression.* London: Hutchinson.

———. 1991. "Les origins du mouvement de la libération des femmes en France." *Nouvelles questions féministes,* no. 16–17–18: 137–48.

Deudon, Catherine. 2003. *Un Mouvement à soi: Images du mouvement des femmes, 1970–2001.* Paris: Éditions Syllepse.

Dhavernas, Odile. 1979. *Droits des femmes, pouvoir des hommes.* Paris: Le Seuil.

Diamond, Irene, and Lee Quinby. 1984. "American Feminism in the Age of the Body." *Signs: Journal of Women in Culture and Society* 14, no. 1: 119–25.

Dijkstra, Sandra. 1980. "Simone de Beauvoir and Betty Friedan: The Politics of Omission." *Feminist Studies* 6, no. 2 (Summer): 290–303.

Duby, Georges, and Michelle Perrot. 1991. *Histoire des femmes en Occident.* Paris: Plon.

Duchen, Claire. 1986. *Feminism in France from May '68 to Mitterand.* London: Routledge and Kegan Paul.

———. 1994. *Women's Rights and Women's Lives in France, 1944–1968.* London: Routledge.

Dumont, Gérard-François. 2002. "Le nombre véritable des avortements." *PanoramiqueS*, no. 60: 61–68.

Dumont, Gérard-François, and J. Legrand. 1981. "Evolution rédente de nombre des décès déclarés dus à l'avortement." *Population* 36, no. 2: 410–14.

Duroi, Nicole, and Maryse Wolinski. 1979. "L'avortement: La campagne est ouverte." *Elle*, no. 1760 (October 1): 112–21.

Ehrenreich, Barbara, and Deirdre English. 1978. *For Her Own Good: 150 Years of the Experts' Advice to Women.* New York: Doubleday.

Eisenstein, Zillah R. 1981. *The Radical Future of Liberalism.* Boston: Northeastern University Press.

———. 1994. *The Color of Gender: Reimaging Democracy.* Berkeley: University of California Press.

El Yamani, Myriame. 1998. *Médias et féminismes: Minoritaires sans paroles.* Paris: L'Harmattan.

Elle. 1995. *Elle, 1945–1995: Nos cinquante premières années.* Paris: Fillipacchi.

Elshtain, Jean B. 1981. *Public Man, Private Woman: Women in Social and Political Thought.* Princeton, NJ: Princeton University Press.

Engeli, Isabelle. 2009. "The Challenges of Abortion and Assisted Reproductive Technologies Policies in Europe." *Comparative European Politics* 7, no. 1: 56–74.

Ezekiel, Judith. 2002. "Le Women's Lib: Made in France." *European Journal of Women's Studies* 9, no. 3: 345–61.

Fallaize, Elizabeth. 1988. *The Novels of Simone de Beauvoir.* London: Routledge.

Farrell, Amy E. 1994. "Desire and Consumption: Women's Magazines in the 1980s." *American Quarterly* 46, no. 4 (December): 621–28.

———. 1998. *Yours in Sisterhood: "Ms." Magazine and the Promise of Popular Feminism.* Chapel Hill: University of North Carolina Press.

Fauré, Christine. 1985. *La Démocratie sans les femmes: Essai sur le libéralisme en France.* Paris: Presses Universitaires de France.

Featherstone, Mike. 1991. "The Body in Consumer Culture." In *The Body: Social Process and Cultural Theory*, edited by Mike Featherstone, Mike Hepworth, and Bryan S. Turner. London: Sage.

Ferguson, Marjorie. 1983. *Forever Feminine: Women's Magazines and the Cult of Femininity.* London: Heinemann.

Ferrand, Michèle, and Maryse Jaspard. 1987. *L'Interruption volontaire de grossesse.* Paris: Presses Universitaires de France.

Fishwick, Sarah. 1999–2000. "Reassessing Beauvoir's Account of the Body in *Le Deuxième Sexe*." *Simone de Beauvoir Studies* 16: 55–68.

———. 2002. *The Body in the Work of Simone de Beauvoir.* Oxford, UK: P. Lang.

Flaubert, Gustave. (1896) 1995. *Madame Bovary.* London: Penguin.

Foley, Susan K. 2004. *Women in France since 1789: The Meanings of Difference.* New York: Palgrave Macmillan.

Foucault, Michel. 1990. *The Use of Pleasure: The History of Sexuality, Volume 2.* Translated by Robert Hurley. New York: Vintage Books. Originally published in French as *L'Usage des plaisirs* (Paris: Gallimard, 1984).

Fourier, Charles. (1841) 1967. *Théorie des quatre mouvements et des destinées générales.* Paris: J.-J. Pauvert.

Frader, Laura Levine. 2008. *Breadwinners and Citizens: Gender in the Making of the French Social Model.* Durham, NC: Duke University Press.

Frader, Laura Levine, and Sonya O. Rose, eds. 1996. *Gender and Class in Modern Europe.* Ithaca, NY: Cornell University Press.

Fraisse, Geneviève. 1994. *Reason's Muse: Sexual Difference and the Birth of Democracy.* Translated by Jane Marie Todd. Chicago: University of Chicago Press. Originally published in French as *Muse de la raison* (Aix-en-Provence: Alinéa, 1989).

Fraser, Nancy. 1989. *Unruly Practices: Power, Discourse, and Gender in Contemporary Social Theory.* Minneapolis: University of Minnesota Press.

Freeman, Jo. 2006. "The Origins of the Women's Liberation Movement." In *The U.S. Women's Movement in Global Perspective,* edited by Lee Ann Banaszak. Lanham, MD: Rowman and Littlefield.

Fuss, Diana. 1992. "Fashion and the Homospectorial Look." *Critical Inquiry* 18 (Summer): 713–37.

Garcia, Sandrine. 2005. "Expertise scientifique et capital militant: Le rôle des médicines dans la lutte pour la légalisation de l'avortement." *Actes de la recherche en sciences sociales* 3, no. 158: 96–115.

Gaspard, Françoise, Claude Servan-Schreiber, and Anne Le Gall. 1992. *Au Pouvoir citoyennes! Liberté, égalité, parité.* Paris: Seuil.

Gatens, Moira. 1996. *Imaginary Bodies: Ethics, Power and Corporeality.* London: Routledge.

Gerassi, John. 1976. "The Second Sex 25 Years Later: Interview with Simone de Beauvoir." *Society* 13, no. 2 (January–February): 79–85.

Giroud, Françoise. 1972. *Si je mens . . . Conversations avec Claude Glayman.* Paris: Stock.

GIS (Groupe Information Santé). 1974. *La Médicine désordonnée: D'une pratique de l'avortement á la lutte pour la santé.* Paris: Solin.

Githens, Marianne, and Dorothy McBride Stetson. 1996. *Abortion Politics: Public Policy in Cross-Cultural Perspective.* New York: Routledge.

Godineau, Dominique. 1988. *Citoyennes tricoteuses: Les femmes du peuple à Paris pendant la Révolution française.* Aix-en-Provence: Alinéa.

———. 1990. "Masculine and Feminine Political Practice during the French Revolution, 1793–Year III." In *Women and Politics in the Age of the Democratic Revolution,* edited by Harriet B. Applewhite and Darline G. Levy. Ann Arbor: University of Michigan Press.

Goodman, Dena. 1994. *The Republic of Letters: A Cultural History of the French Enlightenment.* Ithaca, NY: Cornell University Press.

Gouges, Olympe de. (1791) 1979. "The Rights of Women." In *Women in Revolutionary Paris, 1789–1795: Selected Documents*, translated with notes and commentary by Darline Gay Levy, Harriet Branson Applewhite, and Mary Durham Johnson. Champaign: University of Illinois Press.

Granger, Anne-Marie, and Josette Desbois. 1987. "L'Aventure de la presse féministe." *Cahiers du féminisme* 41/42: 22–25.

Grosz, Elizabeth. 1994. *Volatile Bodies: Toward a Corporeal Feminism.* Bloomington: Indiana University Press.

Guichard, Marie-Thérèse. 1982. "Il ose dire: 'Si j'etais une femme, je ne prendrais pas la pilule.'" *Elle*, no. 1881 (January 25): 7–12.

Gullickson, Gay L. 1992. "The Unruly Women of the Paris Commune." In *Gendered Domains: Rethinking Public and Private in Women's History,* edited by Dorothy O. Helly and Susan M. Reverby. Ithaca, NY: Cornell University Press.

Gunther-Canada, Wendy. 2001. *Rebel Writer: Mary Wollstonecraft and Enlightenment Politics.* DeKalb: Northern Illinois University Press.

Habermas, Jürgen. 1973. *Legitimationsprobleme im Spätkapitalismus.* Frankfurt: Suhrkamp.

———. 1992. *The Structural Transformation of the Public Sphere: An Inquiry into a Category of Bourgeois Society.* Translated by Thomas Burger. Cambridge, MA: MIT Press. Originally published in German as *Strukturwandel der Öffentlichkeit* (Frankfurt a.M.: Suhrkamp, 1990).

Halberstam, Judith. 1998. *Female Masculinity.* Durham, NC: Duke University Press.

Hall, Stuart, and Tony Jefferson, eds. 1976. *Resistance through Rituals.* London: Hutchinson.

Hanley, Sarah, and Marie Denizard. 1994. *Les Droits des femmes et la loi salique.* Paris: Indigo and Côte-femmes.

Hassou, Danielle. 1997. "Histoire de la legislation de la contraception et de l'avortement en France." In *L'Interruption de grossesse depuis la loi Veil: Bilan et perspectives,* edited by Paul Cesbron. Paris: Flammarion Médicine-Sciences.

Hawkesworth, M. E. 1990. *Beyond Oppression: Feminist Theory and Political Strategy.* New York: Continuum.

Hazan, Marie. 1986. "L'avortement et contraception dans la presse féminine française entre 1961 et 1964." Ph.D. diss., University of Montreal.

Heinämaa, Sara. 2003. "The Body as Instrument and Expression." In *The Cambridge Companion to Simone de Beauvoir,* edited by Claudia Card. Cambridge, UK: Cambridge University Press.

Henderson, Sarah L., and Alana S. Jeydel. 2007. *Participation and Protest: Women and Politics in a Global World.* New York: Oxford University Press.

Hennessey, Rosemary. 1993. *Materialist Feminism and the Politics of Discourse.* New York: Routledge.

Hermes, Joke. 1995. *Reading Women's Magazines.* Cambridge, UK: Polity Press.

Hertz, Neil. 1983. "Medusa's Head: Male Hysteria under Political Pressure." *Representations* 4: 27–54.

Hesse, Carla. 2002. *The Other Enlightenment: How French Women Became Modern.* Princeton, NJ: Princeton University Press.

Holland, Alison T. 1998–99. "Simone de Beauvoir's Writing Practice: Madness, Enumeration and Repetition in *Les Belles Images.*" *Simone de Beauvoir Studies* 15: 113–25.

Holveck, Eleanore. 2002. *Simone de Beauvoir's Philosophy of Lived Experience: Literature and Metaphysics.* Lanham, MD: Rowman and Littlefield.

Hufton, Olwen H. 1992. *Women and the Limits of Citizenship in the French Revolution.* Toronto: University of Toronto Press.

Hulbert, Ann. 2003. *Raising America: Experts, Parents, and a Century of Advice about Children.* New York: Knopf.

Hunt, Lynn. 1992. *The Family Romance of the French Revolution.* Berkeley: University of California Press.

———. 1994. "Male Virtue and Republican Motherhood." In *The French Revolution and the Creation of Modern Political Culture,* vol. 4: *The Terror,* edited by Keith M. Baker. Oxford: Pergamon Press.

———. 1996. *The French Revolution and Human Rights: A Brief Documentary History.* Boston: Bedford/St. Martin's Press.

Jardine, Alice. 1979. "Interview with Simone de Beauvoir." *Signs: Journal of Women in Culture and Society* 5, no. 2: 224–36.

Jardine, Alice, and Anne M. Menke, eds. 1991. *Shifting Scenes: Interviews on Women, Writing, and Politics in Post-'68 France.* New York: Columbia University Press.

Jenkins, Henry. 1992. *Textual Poachers: Television Fans and Participatory Culture.* New York: Routledge.

Jenson, Jane. 1986. "Gender and Reproduction, or, Babies and the State." *Studies in Political Economy* 20 (Summer): 9–46.

———. 1987. "Changing Discourses, Changing Agendas: Political Rights and Reproductive Policies in France." In *The Women's Movements of the United States and Western Europe,* edited by Mary Fainsod Katzenstein and Carol McClurg Mueller. Philadelphia: Temple University Press.

Jenson, Jane, and Mariette Sineau. 1994. *Mitterand et les françaises: Un rendez-vous manqué.* Paris: Presses de Science Po.

Jones, Jennifer. 1996. "*Coquettes* and *Grisette:* Women Buying and Selling in Ancient Régime France." In *The Sex of Things: Gender and Consumption in Historical Perspective,* edited by Victoria de Grazia and Ellen Furlough. Berkeley: University of California Press.

Jones, Kathleen B. 1990. "Citizenship in a Woman-Friendly Polity." *Signs: Journal of Women in Culture and Society* 15, no. 4 (Summer): 781–812.

Jordanova, Ludmilla J. 1982. "1789: Reading, Writing, Revolution." In *Proceedings from the Essex Conference on the Sociology of Literature,* edited by Francis Barker. Colchester: University of Essex Press.

Kale, Steven. 2004. *French Salons: High Society and Political Sociability from the Old Regime to the Revolution of 1848.* Baltimore, MD: Johns Hopkins University Press.

Kandel, Liliane. 1979. "La presse féministe aujourd'hui: Des journaux et des femmes." *Pénélope,* no. 1: 44–71.

Kaufmann-McCall, Dorothy. 1983. "Politics of Difference: The Women's Movement in France from May 1968 to Mitterand." *Signs: Journal of Women in Culture and Society* 9, no. 2: 282–93.

Kerber, Linda K. 1988. "Separate Spheres, Female Worlds, Woman's Place: The Rhetoric of Women's History." *Journal of American History* 75, no. 1: 9–39.

Klejman, Laurence, and Florence Rochefort. 1984. "Les associations féministes en France de 1871 à 1914." *Pénélope,* no. 11: 147–53.

———. 1989. *L'Égalité en marche: Le féminisme sous la Troisième République.* Paris: Presse de la fondation nationale des sciences politiques; des femmes.

Kruks, Sonia. 2005. "Simone de Beauvoir and the Politics of Privilege." *Hypatia* 20, no. 1 (Winter): 178–205.

Kulawik, Teresa. 2009. "Staking the Frame of a Feminist Discursive Institutionalism." *Politics & Gender* 5, no. 2: 262–71.

Landes, Joan. B. 1988. *Women and the Public Sphere in the Age of the French Revolution.* Ithaca, N.Y.: Cornell University Press.

———. 1998. "Public and Private Sphere: A Feminist Reconsideration." In *Feminism, the Public and the Private,* edited by Joan B. Landes. New York: Oxford University Press.

Latour, Patricia, Monique Houssin, and Madia Tovar. 1995. *Femmes et citoyennes: Du droit du vote à l'exercice du pouvoir.* Paris: Les Éditions de l'Atélier.

Laubier, Claire, ed. 1990. *The Condition of Women in France, 1945 to the Present: A Documentary Anthology.* London: Routledge.

Le Bras-Chopard, Armelle, and Janine Mossuz-Lavau, eds. 1997. *Les Femmes et la politique.* Paris: L'Harmattan.

Le Doeuff, Michèle. 1980. "Simone de Beauvoir and Existentialism." *Feminist Studies* 6, no. 2 (Summer): 277–89.

Lefèbvre, Edwige L. 2003. "Republicanism and Universalism: Factors of Inclusion and Exclusion in the French Concept of Citizenship." *Citizenship Studies* 7, no. 1: 15–36.

Léger, Danièle. 1982. *Le Féminisme en France.* Paris: Le Sycomore.

Levy, Darline G., and Harriet B. Applewhite. 1990. "Women, Radicalization, and the Fall of the French Monarchy." In *Women and Politics in the Age of the Democratic Revolution,* edited by Harriet B. Applewhite and Darline G. Levy. Ann Arbor: University of Michigan Press.

———. 1992. "Women and Militant Citizenship in Revolutionary Paris." In *Rebel Daughters: Women and the French Revolution,* edited by Sarah E. Melzer and Leslie W. Rabine. Oxford, UK: Oxford University Press.

Lewis, Reina. 1997. "Looking Good: The Lesbian Gaze and Fashion Imagery." *Feminist Review* 55 (Spring): 92–109.

Lipovetsky, Gilles. 1977. *La Troisième femme: Permanence et révolution du féminin.* Paris: Gallimard.

Lister, Ruth. 1997. *Citizenship: Feminist Perspectives.* New York: New York University Press.

Lorde, Audre. 1984. *Sister Outsider: Essays and Speeches.* Trumansburg, NY: Crossing Press.

Lovenduski, Joni, ed. 2005. *State Feminism and Political Representation.* Cambridge, UK: Cambridge University Press.

Lyshaug, Brenda. 2006. "Solidarity without 'Sisterhood'? Feminism and the Ethics of Coalition Building." *Politics & Gender* 2, no. 1: 77–100.

MacIntyre, Alisdair. 1981. *After Virtue: A Study in Moral Theory.* Notre Dame, IN: University of Notre Dame Press.

Mackenzie, Catriona. 1986. "Simone de Beauvoir: Philosophy and/or the Body." In *Feminist Challenges: Social and Political Theory,* edited by Carol Pateman and Elizabeth Grosz. Boston: Northeastern University Press.

Macpherson, C. B. 1962. *The Political Theory of Possessive Individualism: Hobbes to Locke.* Oxford, UK: Oxford University Press.

Maillard, Claude. 1974. *Avortement: Les Pièces du dossier.* Paris: Éditions Robert Laffont.

Marand-Fouquet, Catherine. 1989. *La Femme au temps de la Révolution française.* Paris: Stock.

Marso, Lori Jo. 1999. *(Un)Manly Citizens: Jean-Jacques Rousseau's and Germaine de Staël's Subversive Women.* Baltimore: Johns Hopkins University Press.

———. 2006. *Feminist Thinkers and the Demands of Femininity: The Lives and Work of Intellectual Women.* New York: Routledge.

Marso, Lori Jo, and Patricia Moynagh. 2006. "Introduction: A Radical Approach to Political Thinking." In *Simone de Beauvoir's Political Thinking,* edited by Lori Jo Marso and Patricia Moynagh. Urbana: University of Illinois Press.

Martel, Frédéric. 1999. *The Pink and the Black: Homosexuals in France since 1968.* Stanford, CA: Stanford University Press.

Mauduit, Jean. 1988. "La femme vingst ans après." *Elle,* no. 2195 (February 1): 7.

Mazur, Amy G. 1995. "Strong State and Symbolic Reform: The Ministère des droits de la femme in France." In *Comparative State Feminisms,* edited by Dorothy McBride Stetson and Amy G. Mazur. Thousand Oaks, CA: Sage Publications.

———. 2001. *State Feminism, Women's Movements, and Job Training: Making Democracies Work in the Global Economy.* New York: Routledge.

———. 2005. "Gendering the Fifth Republic." In *Developments in French Politics 3,* edited by Alistair Cole, Patrick Le Gales, and Jonah Levy. London: Palgrave Macmillan.

McBride Stetson, Dorothy. 1987. *Women's Rights in France.* Westport, CT: Greenwood Press.

McBride Stetson, Dorothy, and Amy G. Mazur, eds. 1995. *Comparative State Feminisms.* Thousand Oaks, CA: Sage Publications.

McCracken, Ellen. 1993. *Decoding Women's Magazines: From "Mademoiselle" to "Ms."* Houndmills, UK: Macmillan.

McDonald, Katrina Bell. 2006. *Embracing Sisterhood: Class, Identity and Contemporary Black Women.* Lanham, MD: Rowman and Littlefield.

McMillan, James F. 1981. *Housewife or Harlot: The Place of Women in French Society, 1870–1940.* New York: St. Martin's Press.

Melder, Keith E. 1977. *Beginnings of Sisterhood: The American Woman's Rights Movement, 1800–1850.* New York: Schocken Books.

Melzer, Sarah E., and Kathryn Norberg, eds. 1998. *From the Royal to the Republican Body: Incorporating the Political in Seventeenth- and Eighteenth-Century France.* Berkeley: University of California Press.

Melzer, Sara E., and Leslie W. Rabine. 1992. *Rebel Daughters: Women and the French Revolution.* New York: Oxford University Press.

MFPF (Mouvement français pour le planning familial). 2005. *Statistiques France.* Paris: MFPF.

Michel, Andrée, and Geneviève Texier. 1964. *La Condition de la française d'aujourd'hui.* Vol. 2: *Les groupes de pression: Perspectives nouvelles.* Geneva: Éditions Gonthier.

Milan Women's Bookstore Collective. 1990. *Sexual Difference: A Theory of Social-Symbolic Practice.* Bloomington: Indiana University Press.

Miller, Michael B. 1981. *The Bon Marché: Bourgeois Culture and the Department Store, 1869–1920.* Princeton, NJ: Princeton University Press.

MLF. 1971. "Je me suis fait avorter." *Le Nouvel Observateur,* no. 334 (April 5). http://

tempsreel.nouvelobs.com/actualites/societe/20071127.OBS7018/le_manifeste_des_343_salopes_paru_dans_le_nouvel_obs_en.html (accessed January 31, 2010).

Moi, Toril. 1985. *Sexual/Textual Politics: Feminist Literary Theory.* London: Methuen.

———. 1986. "Existentialism and Feminism: The Rhetoric of Biology in *The Second Sex.*" *Oxford Literary Review* 8 (June): 88–95.

———. 1994. *Simone de Beauvoir: The Making of an Intellectual Woman.* Oxford: Blackwell.

Monteil, Claudine. 1997. "Simone de Beauvoir and the Women's Movement in France: An Eye-Witness Account." *Simone de Beauvoir Studies* 14: 6–12.

Montesquieu, Charles de Secondat, Baron de. 1874. *De L'ésprit des lois.* Paris: Garnier Frères.

Morgan, Robin. 1970. *Sisterhood Is Powerful: An Anthology of Writings from the Women's Liberation Movement.* New York: Random House.

———. 1984. *Sisterhood Is Global: The International Women's Movement Anthology.* Garden City, NY: Anchor Books.

———. 2003. *Sisterhood Is Forever: The Women's Anthology for a New Millennium.* New York: Washington Square Press.

Moscovici, Claudia. 2000. *Gender and Citizenship: The Dialectics of Subject-Citizenship in Nineteenth-Century French Literature and Culture.* Lanham, MD: Rowman and Littlefield.

Moses, Claire Goldberg. 1984. *French Feminism in the Nineteenth Century.* Albany: State University of New York Press.

Mossuz-Lavau, Janine. 1986. "Abortion Politics in France under the Governments of the Right and the Left (1973–1984)." In *The New Politics of Abortion,* edited by Joni Lovenduski and Joyce Outshoorn. London: Sage Publications.

———. 1999. "Les Parliamentaires et la 'libération sexuelle.'" In *Un Siècle d'antiféminisme,* edited by Christine Bard. Paris: Fayard.

Mossuz-Lavau, Janine, and Mariette Sineau. 1983. *Enquête sur les femmes et la politique en France.* Paris: Presses Universitaires de France.

Mouffe, Chantal. 1992. "Feminism, Citizenship, and Radical Democratic Politics." In *Feminists Theorize the Political,* edited by Judith Butler and Joan W. Scott. New York: Routledge.

Mulvey, Laura. 1975. "Visual Pleasure and Narrative Cinema." *Screen* 16, no. 3: 6–18.

Offen, Karen. 1988. "Defining Feminism: A Historical Comparative Approach." *Signs: Journal of Women in Culture and Society* 14, no. 1: 119–57.

———. 1990. "The New Sexual Politics of French Revolutionary Historiography." *French Historical Studies* 16, no. 4 (Fall): 909–22.

———. 1994. "Women, Citizenship and Suffrage with a French Twist." In *Suffrage and Beyond: International Feminist Perspectives,* edited by Caroline Daley and Melanie Nolan. Auckland, NZ: Auckland University Press.

———. 2003. "Review: French Women's History: Retrospect (1789–1940) and Prospect." *French Historical Studies* 26, no. 4 (Autumn): 727–67.

Okin, Susan Moller. 1979. *Women in Western Political Thought.* Princeton, NJ: Princeton University Press.

Orloff, Ann Shola. 1993. "Gender and the Social Rights of Citizenship: The Comparative Analysis of Gendered Relations and Welfare States." *American Sociological Review* 58, no. 3 (June): 303–28.

Outram, Dorinda. 1989. *The Body and the French Revolution: Sex, Class, and Political Culture.* New Haven, CT: Yale University Press.

Parkins, Wendy. 2000. "Protesting Like a Girl: Embodiment, Dissent, and Feminist Agency." *Feminist Theory* 1, no. 1: 59–78.

———, ed. 2002. *Fashioning the Body Politic: Dress, Gender, Citizenship.* Oxford: Berg.

Pateman, Carol. 1987. "Feminist Critiques of the Public/Private Dichotomy." In *Feminism and Equality,* edited by Anne Phillips. New York: New York University Press.

———. 1988. *The Sexual Contract.* Stanford, CA: Stanford University Press.

Patterson, Yolanda A. 1986. "Simone de Beauvoir and the Demystification of Motherhood." *Yale French Studies* 72: 87–105.

———. 1989. "Mothers, Daughters, and Kim Chernin's Theories of Eating Disorders in the Fictional Works of Simone de Beauvoir." *Simone de Beauvoir Studies* 6: 40–48.

Patton, Cindy, and Robert L. Caserio. 2000. "Introduction: Citizenship 2000." *Cultural Studies* 14, no. 1: 1–14.

Penrod, Lynn Kettler. 1987. "Consuming Woman Consumed: Images of Consumer Society in Simone de Beauvoir's *Les Belles Images* and Christiane Rochefort's *Les Stances à Sophie.*" *Simone de Beauvoir Studies* 4: 159–75.

Petchesky, Rosalind Pollack. 1995. "The Body as Property: A Feminist Re-vision." In *Conceiving the New World Order: The Global Politics of Reproduction,* edited by Faye D. Ginsburg and Rayna Rapp. Berkeley: University of California Press.

Phillips, Anne, ed. 1987. *Feminism and Equality.* New York: New York University Press.

———. 1991. *Engendering Democracy.* University Park, Pa.: Pennsylvania State University Press.

Picq, Françoise. 1993. *Libération des femmes: Les années-mouvement.* Paris: Seuil.

Pipher, Mary. 1997. *Hunger Pains: The Modern Woman's Tragic Quest for Thinness.* New York: Ballantine Books.

Pisano, Laura. 2002. "Histoire du journalisme, histoire des femmes: Thèmes et methods." In *Les Femmes dans l'espace public: Itinéraires français et italiens,* edited by Christiane Veauvy. Paris: Éditions de la Maison de Sciences de l'Homme.

Preston, Larry. 1995. "Theorizing Difference: Voices From the Margins." *American Political Science Review* 89, no. 4 (December): 941–53.

Pringle, Colombe. 1995. *Telles qu'Elle: Cinquante ans d'histoire des femmes à travers le journal Elle.* Paris: Bernard Grasset.

Quinlan, Sean M. 2007. *The Great Nation in Decline: Sex, Modernity and Health Crises in Revolutionary France, c. 1750–1850.* Burlington, VT: Ashgate.

Rawls, John. 1971. *A Theory of Justice.* Cambridge, MA: Harvard University Press.

Redstocking Sister. 1971. "Consumerism and Women." In *Woman in Sexist Society: Studies in Power and Powerlessness,* edited by Vivian Gornick and Barbara K. Moran. New York: Basic Books.

Reineke, Sandra. 2008–2009. "Border Crossings: Simone de Beauvoir, Feminist Intellectual Exchanges, and the Organization of Women's Studies Programs in France, Germany, and the United States." *Simone de Beauvoir Studies* 25: 63–79.

Remy, Monique. 1990. *Histoire des mouvements des femmes: De l'utopie à l'intégration.* Paris: L'Harmattan.

Renaudin, Marie. 1984. "RU 486: La pilule d'après." *Elle*, no. 2032 (December 17): 62–65.

———. 1988a. "RU 486: La pilule qui change tout." *Elle*, no. 2195 (February 1): 46–49.

———. 1988b. "RU 486: L'avortement en comprimés."*Elle*, no. 2232 (October 17): 130–31.

Renaudin, Marie, and Marie-Aline Janneau. 1985. "L'amour donnerait le cancer? Des médecins répondent." *Elle*, no. 2072 (September 23): 90–91.

"Respect du corps: Les solutions Warner." 1983. *Elle*, no. 1946 (April 25): 12.

Reynolds, Siân. 1987. "Marianne's Citizens? Women, the Republic and Universal Suffrage in France." In *Women, State, and Revolution: Essays on Power and Gender in Europe since 1789*, edited by Siân Reynolds. Amherst: University of Massachusetts Press.

Riot-Sarcey, Michèle. 1995. *Démocratie et répresentation: Actes du colloque d'Albi des 19 et 20 novembre 1994.* Paris: Kimé.

Rivoire and Carret. 1986. Advertisement. *Elle*, no. 2095 (March 3): 122–23.

Roberts, Marie Louise. 1994. *Civilization without Sexes: Reconstructing Gender in Postwar France, 1917–1927.* Chicago: University of Chicago Press.

Robinson, Jean C. 2001. "Gendering the Abortion Debate: The French Case." In *Abortion Politics, Women's Movements, and the Democratic State: A Comparative Study of State Feminism*, edited by Dorothy McBride Stetson. Oxford, UK: Oxford University Press.

Roche, Daniel. 1998. *France in the Enlightenment.* Translated by Arthur Goldhammer. Cambridge, MA: Harvard University Press. Originally published in French as *La France des Lumières* (Paris: Gallimard, 1993).

Rogers, Adrienne. 1984. "Women and the Law." In *French Women and the Age of Enlightenment*, edited by Samia I. Spencer. Bloomington: Indiana University Press.

Rosa, Annette. 1988. *Citoyennes: Les femmes et la Révolution française.* Paris: Messidor.

Rosen, Ruth. 2000. *The World Split Open: How the Modern Women's Movement Changed America.* New York: Viking Press.

Ross, Kristin. 1995. *Fast Cars, Clean Bodies: Decolonization and the Reordering of French Culture.* Cambridge, MA: MIT Press.

Rousseau, Jean-Jacques. (1762) 1920. *"The Social Contract" and "Discourses."* Translated with an Introduction by G. D. H. Cole. New York: E. P. Dutton. Originally published in French as *Du Contrat social* (Amsterdam: Chez Marc-Michel Rey, 1762).

Rowbotham, Sheila. 1992. *Women in Movement: Feminism and Social Action.* New York: Routledge.

Rudder, Chantal de. 1980. "Qui a peur du MLF?" *Elle*, no. 1787 (April 7): 6–12.

Ruhl, Lealle. 2002. "Dilemmas of the Will: Uncertainty, Reproduction, and the Rhetoric of Control." *Signs: Journal of Women in Culture and Society* 27, no. 3: 641–63.

Sánchez, Lucía Gómez, and Ana Belén Sevillano. 2006. "Experience, Subjectivity and Politics in the Italian Feminist Movement: Redefining the Boundaries between Body and Discourse." *European Journal of Women's Studies* 13, no. 4: 343–55.

Sandel, Michael J. 1982. *Liberalism and the Limits of Justice.* Cambridge, UK: Cambridge University Press.

Sandrel, Carol. 1989. "La liberté menacée." *Elle*, no. 2250 (February 20): 70–71.

Sapiro, Virginia. 1992. *A Vindication of Political Virtue: The Political Theory of Mary Wollstonecraft.* Chicago: University of Chicago Press.

Sarde, Michèle. 1983. *Regard sur les Françaises, Xe siècle–XXe siècle.* Paris: Stock.

Sartre, Jean-Paul. (1938) 1968. *La Nausée.* Paris: Gallimard.

Savarsy, Wendy. 1997. "Social Citizenship from a Feminist Perspective." *Hypatia* 12, no. 4 (Fall): 54–73.

Scanlon, Jennifer. 1995. *Inarticulate Longings: The Ladies' Home Journal, Gender, and the Promises of Consumer Culture.* New York: Routledge.

Scarth, Fredrika. 2004. *The Other Within: Ethics, Politics, and the Body in Simone de Beauvoir.* Lanham, MD: Rowman and Littlefield.

Schiebinger, Londa. 1993. *Nature's Body: Gender in the Making of Modern Science.* Boston: Beacon Press.

Schwarzer, Alice. 1984. *After "The Second Sex": Conversations with Simone de Beauvoir.* New York: Pantheon Books.

Scott, Joan W. 1988. "Deconstructing Equality-versus-Difference: Or, the Uses of Poststructuralist Theory for Feminism." *Feminist Studies* 14, no. 1 (Spring): 33–50.

———. 1996. *Only Paradoxes to Offer: French Feminists and the Rights of Man.* Cambridge, MA: Harvard University Press.

———. 2005. *Parité! Sexual Equality and the Crisis of French Universalism.* Chicago: Chicago University Press.

Ségal, Marcelle. 1987. "Courrier du coeur." *Elle*, no. 2148 (March 9): 242.

Shelby, Karen. 2006. "Beauvoir and Ethical Responsibility." In *Simone de Beauvoir's Political Thinking,* edited by Lori Jo Marso and Patricia Moynagh. Urbana: University of Illinois Press.

Shklar, Judith N. 1991. *American Citizenship: The Quest for Inclusion.* Cambridge, MA: Harvard University Press.

Siim, Birte. 2000. *Gender and Citizenship: Politics and Agency in France, Britain and Denmark.* Cambridge, UK: Cambridge University Press.

Simons, Margaret A. 1995. "*The Second Sex*: From Marxism to Radical Feminism." In *Feminist Interpretations of Simone de Beauvoir,* edited by Margaret A. Simons. University Park: Pennsylvania State University Press.

———. 1999. *Beauvoir and "The Second Sex": Feminism, Race, and the Origins of Existentialism.* Lanham, MD: Rowman and Littlefield.

Sineau, Mariette. 1988. *Des Femmes en politique.* Paris: Economica.

———. 1997. "La parité à la Française: Un contre-modèl de l'égalité républicaine?" In *Les Femmes et la politique,* edited by Armelle Le Bras-Chopard and Janine Mossuz-Lavau. Paris: L'Harmattan.

Skinner, Quentin. 1978. *The Foundations of Modern Political Thought.* Cambridge, UK: Cambridge University Press.

Smith, Bonnie G. 1981. *Ladies of the Leisure Class: The Bourgeoises of Northern France in the Nineteenth Century.* Princeton, NJ: Princeton University Press.

Soprani, Anne. 1989. *La Révolution et les femmes, 1789–1796.* Paris: MA Éditions.

Soriano, Véronique. 1982. "Après l'avortement: Regret, soulagement, remords." *Elle*, no. 1878 (January 4): 6–13.

Sparks, Holloway. 1997. "Dissident Citizenship: Democratic Theory, Political Courage, and Activist Women." *Hypatia* 12, no. 4: 75–109.

Stanley, Adam C. 2008. *Modernizing Tradition: Gender and Consumerism in Interwar France and Germany.* Baton Rouge: Louisiana State University Press.

Stevenson, Nick, ed. 2001. *Culture and Citizenship.* London: Sage Publications.

Stewart, Danièle. 1980. "The Women's Movement in France." *Signs: Journal of Women in Culture and Society* 6, no. 2: 350–54.

Stewart, Mary Lynn. 2001. *For Health and Beauty: Physical Culture for Frenchwomen, 1880s–1930s.* Baltimore: Johns Hopkins University Press.

Storey, John. 1996. *Cultural Studies and the Study of Popular Culture.* Athens: University of Georgia Press.

Sullerot, Evelyne. 1963. *La Presse féminine.* Paris: A. Colin.

Swingewood, Alan. 1977. *The Myth of Mass Culture.* London: Macmillan.

Taylor, Charles. 1989. *Sources of the Self: The Making of the Modern Identity.* Cambridge, MA: Harvard University Press.

Tidd, Ursula. 1999. *Simone de Beauvoir, Gender and Testimony.* Cambridge, UK: Cambridge University Press.

———. 2005. "*Les Belles Images:* Continuing the Refusal of History." In *Simone de Beauvoir's Fiction: Women and Language,* edited by Alison T. Holland and Louise Renée. American University Studies 27: Feminist Studies, vol. 10. New York: Peter Lang.

Tiersten, Lisa. 2001. *Marianne in the Market: Envisioning Consumer Society in Fin-de-Siècle France.* Berkeley: University of California Press.

Tilly, Charles. 1995. *Citizenship, Identity and Social History.* Cambridge, UK: Cambridge University Press.

Tournier, Françoise. 1979. "L'avortement: Un dossier noir et blanc." *Elle,* no. 1764 (October 29): 6–24.

———. 1988. "RU 486: Notre affair à tous."*Elle,* no. 2235 (November 7): 7.

Triolet, Elsa. 1959. *Roses à credit.* Paris: Gallimard.

Tristan, Anne, and Annie de Pisan. 1977. *Histoires du M.L.F.* Introduction by Simone de Beauvoir. Paris: Calmann-Lévy.

Turner, Bryan S. 1993. *Citizenship and Social Theory.* London: Sage Publications.

Valk, Anne M. 2008. *Radical Sisters: Second-Wave Feminism and Black Liberation in Washington, D.C.* Urbana: University of Illinois Press.

Veauvy, Christiane, and Laura Pisano. 1997. *Paroles oubliées: Les femmes et la construction de l'état-nation en France et en Italie (1789–1860).* Paris: A. Colin.

Venner, Fiammetta. 1995. *L'Opposition à l'avortement: Du lobby au commando.* Paris: Berg International.

Vintges, Karen. 1995. "*The Second Sex* and Philosophy." In *Feminist Interpretations of Simone de Beauvoir,* edited by Margaret A. Simons. University Park: Pennsylvania State University Press.

Vogel, Ursula. 1988. "Under Permanent Guardianship: Women's Condition under Modern Civil Law." In *The Political Interests of Gender: Developing Theory and Research with a Feminist Face,* edited by Kathleen B. Jones and Anna G. Jónasdóttir. Los Angeles: Sage.

Wadia, Khursheed. 1991. "Women's Magazines: Coming to Terms with Feminism Post–May 1968." *French Cultural Studies* 2, no. 6 (October): 261–74.

Walby, Sylvia. 1994. "Is Citizenship Gendered?" *Sociology* 28, no. 2: 379–95.

Walton, Whitney. 2000. *Eve's Proud Descendants: Four Women Writers and Republican Politics in Nineteenth-Century France.* Stanford, CA: Stanford University Press.

Ward, Julie K. 1995. "Beauvoir's Two Senses of 'Body' in *The Second Sex.*" In *Feminist Interpretations of Simone de Beauvoir,* edited by Margaret A. Simons. University Park: Pennsylvania State University Press.

Weiner, Susan E. 1995. "The *Consommatrice* of the 1950s in Elsa Triolet's *Roses à crédit.*" *French Cultural Studies* 6, no. 17: 123–44.

———. 1999. "Two Modernities: From *Elle* to *Mademoiselle*—Women's Magazines in Postwar France." *Contemporary European History* 8, no. 3: 395–409.

Werbner, Pnina. 1999. "Political Motherhood and the Feminization of Citizenship: Women's Activism and the Transformation of the Public Sphere." In *Women, Citizenship and Difference,* edited by Nira Yuval-Davis and Pnina Werbner. London: Zed Books.

Williams, Rosalind H. 1982. *Dream Worlds: Mass Consumption in Late Nineteenth-Century France.* Berkeley: University of California Press.

Winship, Janice. 1987. *Inside Women's Magazines.* London: Pandora Press.

Wolinski, Maryse. 1980. "*Elle* vous signale." *Elle,* no. 1796 (June 9): 107.

Woliver, Laura R. 2002. *The Political Geographies of Pregnancy.* Urbana: University of Illinois Press.

Yeatman, Anna. 2001. "Feminism and Citizenship." In *Culture and Citizenship,* edited by Nick Stevenson. London: Sage.

Young, Iris Marion. 1990. "Polity and Group Difference: A Critique of the Ideal of Universal Citizenship." In *Feminism and Political Theory,* edited by Cass R. Sunstein. Chicago: University of Chicago Press.

———. 2005. *On Female Body Experience: "Throwing Like a Girl" and Other Essays.* New York: Oxford University Press.

Yuval-Davis, Nira. 1991. "The Citizenship Debate: Women, Ethnic Processes, and the State." *Feminist Review* 39: 58–68.

Yuval-Davis, Nira, and Pnina Werbner, eds. 1999. *Women, Citizenship and Difference.* London: Zed Books.

Zancarini-Fournel, Michelle. 2004. "Les féminismes: Des mouvements autonomes?" In *Le Siècle des féminismes,* edited by Eliane Gubin. Paris: Éditions de l'atelier.

Zerilli, Linda M. G. 2005. *Feminism and the Abyss of Freedom.* Chicago: University of Chicago Press.

Zola, Emile. (1883) 1980. *Au Bonheur des dames.* Paris: Gallimard.

INDEX